Words Every 2nd Grader Needs to Know!

By Lee S. Justice

Frank Schaffer Publications
An imprint of Carson-Dellosa Publishing LLC
Greensboro, North Carolina

Table of Contents

Frank Schaffer Publications
An imprint of Carson-Dellosa Publishing LLC
PO Box 35665
Greensboro, NC 27425 USA

5 6 7 8 PAT 13 12 11 10

ISBN 978-0-76823-552-4
123107800

Dear Educator,

Welcome to *Words Every Second Grader Needs to Know!* This vocabulary series supports and supplements instruction in the content areas. The reproducible pages are designed to give students extra practice in using academic vocabulary. Academic vocabulary includes the subject-specific words that often challenge learners—words such as *larva*, *paragraph*, and *rural*—which they rarely encounter in everyday use. Terms like these may be challenging, but they are also essential to a student's ability to learn new subject concepts.

The 180 words in *Words Every Second Grader Needs to Know!* have been selected to match national education standards in the curriculum areas. The activities feature the vocabulary words in a variety of contexts so that students can actively think about how each word is used and make their own thoughtful connections to them.

Words Every Second Grader Needs to Know! is organized by content area. Start with any content area you wish. Then, provide students with the activity pages in order. An **Introduction Page** starts each section. It features a list of the words in that section, with two blanks before each word. Have students use the rating scale to evaluate their knowledge of each word before they do the activities and then again after completing the activities. **Explore a Word** activities have students focus on one word at a time to create their own associations. **Compare Words** activities show students how two related words are alike and different in meaning. Paired **Make Connections** pages help students understand the relationships among words that are often used together. And **Play With Words** activities provide additional context and review in a playful format.

As students work through the activities, provide opportunities for them to read aloud from the pages and to share ideas about word usage and meaning. Have students explain the reasoning behind their choices. If an activity asks for open-ended responses, encourage variety.

The Student Dictionary pages are organized by content area and support the activity pages in each section. Students may use the Student Dictionary as they work on each activity page. You may also use the Student Dictionary to model and review dictionary skills, such as alphabetical order, pronunciation, and parts of speech. Each section of the Student Dictionary ends with space for students to write more words and meanings from their subject learning.

Reinforce and extend vocabulary knowledge by using the **Game Ideas and Suggestions** section, which includes ideas for the word cards provided at the back of this book, and game templates intended for small group or whole group activities.

We believe that with *Words Every Second Grader Needs to Know!*, your students will be well equipped with the necessary skills for success with academic vocabulary.

Sincerely,
Frank Schaffer Publications

How to Use the Vocabulary Word Cards

Word cards with key vocabulary words are provided at the end of this book. These can be used as flash cards, also called *association cards*, to help students build quick associations between a word and its content-related meaning. Create additional word cards with all of the vocabulary words from this book or with additional words from your students' content-area learning. Incorporate the cards as you teach new vocabulary words. Use the cards to create a word wall. Or select one card and use that word for "Word of the Day" type activities. You can also use the cards for extension games and activities. Below are a few ideas to get you started.

Know, Don't Know

Step 1: Student reads each word and definition in the pile.

Step 2: Student reads each word and tries to say its definition. If correct, the card goes in the "Know" pile. If incorrect, the card goes in the "Don't Know" pile.

Step 3: Student repeats Step 1, using only the "Don't Know" pile cards.

Step 4: Student repeats Step 2, and so on.

Step 5: After correctly defining each word in the original pile, the student tries again several days later.

Quiz Show

Select a quizmaster to read each word or its definition to a panel of three contestants or to two teams of contestants. Each contestant or team has ten seconds to write the definition or the word. If they do so correctly, they earn a point. The winner has the most points at the end of a predetermined time period or number of words.

Guessing Game

Display a selected group of cards, and play "I'm thinking of a word that. . . ." Offer students one clue at a time, including clues about word structure and relationships. Encourage students to raise their hands only when they are "absolutely sure" of the word.

Example for the word *measure*:

- I'm thinking of a word that has to do with height and weight.
- This word has two syllables.
- This word is often used with *miles*, *pounds*, and *tablespoons*.
- This word tells what you do when you use a ruler.
- What's the word?

Encourage students to try their hand at offering clues.

Name ______________________

Important Math Words You Need to Know!

Use this list to keep track of how well you know the new words.

0 = Don't Know   1 = Know It Somewhat   2 = Know It Well

___ ___ add
___ ___ bar graph
___ ___ cent
___ ___ cube
___ ___ difference
___ ___ estimate
___ ___ even number
___ ___ dime
___ ___ dollar
___ ___ measure
___ ___ minus
___ ___ nickel
___ ___ odd number
___ ___ pictograph
___ ___ plus
___ ___ quarter
___ ___ regroup
___ ___ sphere
___ ___ subtract
___ ___ sum

Name ______________________

Explore a Word

estimate—To tell about how many.

Follow each instruction.

1. A school has three second-grade classes. Alicia estimates that there are about 300 second graders in the school. Ruben estimates that there are about 60 second graders. Whose estimate do you think is better? Tell why you think that.

____

____

2. Look at the two amounts below. Circle the one that is an estimate.

$6.32 $6.00

3. Look at the picture. Estimate how many glasses of juice are left in the pitcher. Write your estimate next to the pitcher.

4. Write a sentence with the word *estimate*.

____

____

Name ______________________

Compare Words

even number—A number that can make pairs.

odd number—A number that cannot make pairs.

Write *odd number* or *even number* on each blank.

1. An ______________________

has 1, 3, 5, 7, or 9 in the ones place.

An ______________________

has 0, 2, 4, 6, or 8 in the ones place.

2. Two friends want to share 3 cookies.

An ______________________

of friends want to share an

______________________ of

cookies.

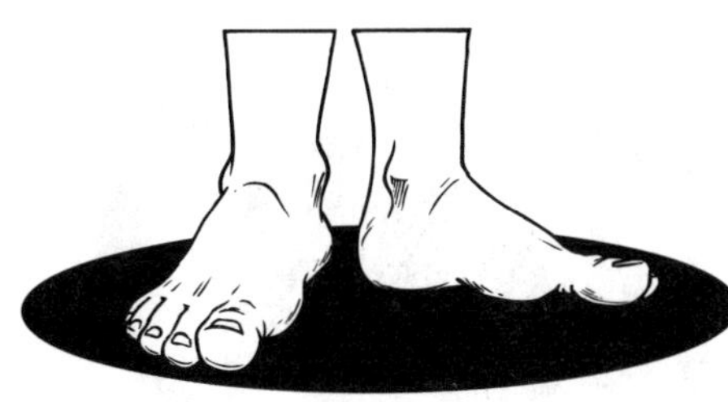

3. A person has an

______________________ of

feet.

A foot has an

______________________ of

toes.

Name ______________________

Compare Words

cube—Six squares of the same size put together to make a box.

sphere—The shape of a ball.

Which pictures show cubes? Which ones show spheres? Write *c* for *cube* or *s* for *sphere*. Cross out the pictures that are not cubes or spheres.

1. ___ 

2. ___ 

3. ___ 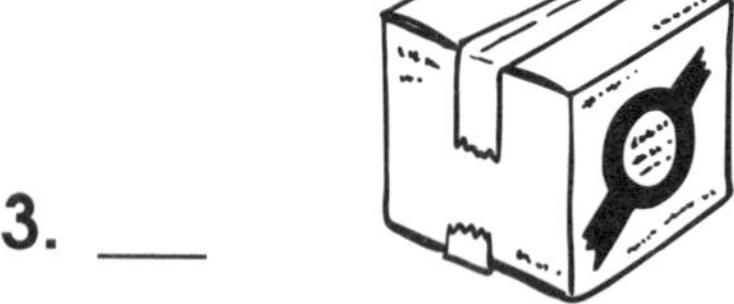

4. ___

5. ___

6. ___

7. ___ 

8. ___ 

9. ___ 

10. ___ 

Name ____________________

Make Connections

add—To put two or more numbers together.

plus—The + sign.

sum—The answer after adding numbers.

Look at the problem. Then, complete each sentence with a vocabulary word.

$$\begin{array}{r} 12 \\ +\underline{17} \\ 29 \end{array}$$

1. The ____________________ sign means "add."
2. We need to ____________________ the ones first.
3. The ____________________ of 2 and 7 is 9.
4. We ____________________ the tens next.
5. The ____________________ of 1 and 1 is 2.
6. Twelve ____________________ seventeen is twenty-nine.

Name ___________________________

Make Connections

add	plus	sum

Read each sentence. Is it correct? Put a ✓ after it. If it is not correct, show how to fix it.

1. The plus sign looks like a star.

2. Add numbers to find the plus.

3. The sum comes after the = sign.

4. Six cookies plus four cookies leaves two cookies.

5. Adding makes a number smaller.

Name ______________________________

Make Connections

subtract—To take away one number from another.

minus—The – sign.

difference—The answer after subtracting.

regroup—To show the same number in a different way.

Look at the problem. Then, complete each sentence with a vocabulary word.

$$\begin{array}{r} 41 \\ -\underline{27} \end{array} \qquad \begin{array}{r} \overset{3}{\cancel{4}}\overset{}{\cancel{1}} \\ -\underline{27} \\ 14 \end{array}$$

1. The ____________________ sign tells us to subtract.
2. We can't ____________________ 7 from 1, because 1 is too small.
3. We'll ____________________ 41 to make 3 tens and 11 ones.
4. Eleven ____________________ seven is four.
5. Next, we ____________________ the tens, 3 – 2.
6. The ____________________ is 14.

Name ______________________

Make Connections

subtract	minus	difference	regroup

Read each sentence. Is it correct? Put a ✓ after it. If it is not correct, show how to fix it.

1. Regroup 1 ten and 9 ones as 19 tens.

2. Ten minus four equals six.

3. Add numbers to find the difference.

4. When you subtract, you take something away.

5. The difference is what is left after subtracting.

Name ______________________

Make Connections

measure—To find out how long, big, or heavy something is.

bar graph—A chart that uses bars to stand for amounts.

pictograph—A chart that uses pictures to stand for amounts.

Look at the graphs to answer the questions.

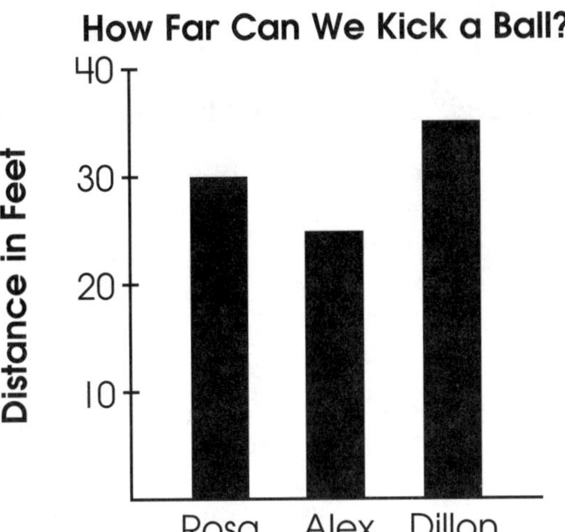

1. How many children chose sliding as their favorite activity? Write the answer and your reason. Use the word *pictograph*.

____

____

2. Which child kicked the farthest? Write the answer and your reason. Use the word *bar graph*.

____

____

3. How do you think the children measured their kicks for the bar graph?

____

____

Name ______________________________

Make Connections

measure	bar graph	pictograph

Read each sentence. Is it correct? Put a ✓ after it. If it is not correct, show how to fix it.

1. A pictograph has pictures that show numbers.

2. You can measure your height with a scale.

3. The shortest bar in a bar graph shows the biggest amount.

4. A bar graph might have one  standing for five people.

5. Use miles to measure the length of a room.

Name ______________________

Make Connections

cent—One penny, written as 1¢ or $.01.

nickel—Five cents, written as 5¢ or $.05.

dime—Ten cents, written as 10¢ or $.10.

quarter—Twenty-five cents, written as 25¢ or $.25.

dollar—One hundred cents, written as $1.00.

Write the vocabulary word that names each picture.

1. ______________________

2. ______________________

3. ______________________

4. ______________________

5. ______________________

6. ______________________

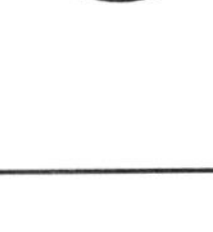

7. ______________________

8. ______________________

9. ______________________

Name ___________________________

Make Connections

cent	nickel	dime	quarter	dollar

Read each sentence. Is it correct? Put a ✓ after it. If it is not correct, show how to fix it.

1. Two nickels and a dime make $.50.

2. One dollar equals four quarters.

3. Seventy-five cents is written $75.00.

4. A dime is worth less than a nickel.

5. Two quarters are the same as three dimes.

Name ______________________

Make Connections

Follow each instruction.

1. Use numbers to show the sum of three nickels and two dimes.

2. How many books did three friends read in a month? Meg read six books, Jaden read nine books, and Rico read seven books. Show the amounts on the bar graph.

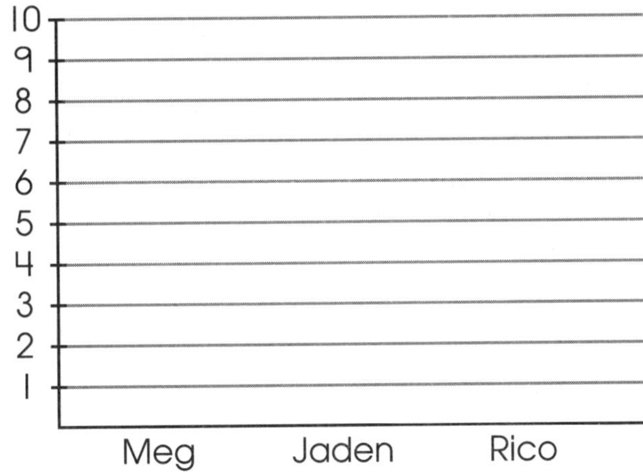

3. Show one way to regroup 5 tens and 4 ones.

4. Read the sentence below. Give an example to show what it means.

   If you subtract 1 from an even number, the difference is an odd number.

5. Use the words *estimate* and *measure* to write about the size of something you see around you.

   ____

   ____

Name ______________________

Play With Words

Code Words

Choose the word that fits in each sentence. Circle its letter.

1. A berry has the shape of a ___.
   - **l** measure
   - **m** cube
   - **n** sphere

2. There are four ___ in a dollar.
   - **u** quarters
   - **v** nickels
   - **w** dimes

3. One nickel ___ two pennies make seven cents.
   - **l** subtract
   - **m** plus
   - **n** quarter

4. Eight ___ four equals four.
   - **a** plus
   - **b** minus
   - **c** add

5. Six squares can make a ___.
   - **c** cent
   - **d** bar graph
   - **e** cube

6. A chart that shows amounts is a ___.
   - **r** pictograph
   - **s** dollar
   - **t** regroup

Write the circled letters in order. You will find the missing word in the message.

You are ______________________ one!

Name ____________________

Important Science and Health Words You Need to Know!

Use this list to keep track of how well you know the new words.

0 = Don't Know   1 = Know It Somewhat   2 = Know It Well

___ ___ amphibian
___ ___ attract
___ ___ breathe
___ ___ constellation
___ ___ flower
___ ___ fruit
___ ___ heart
___ ___ larva
___ ___ life cycle
___ ___ lung
___ ___ magnetic
___ ___ magnify
___ ___ mammal
___ ___ moon
___ ___ muscle
___ ___ offspring
___ ___ oxygen
___ ___ planet
___ ___ pole
___ ___ pump
___ ___ pupa
___ ___ repel
___ ___ reptile
___ ___ root
___ ___ seedling
___ ___ soil
___ ___ solar system
___ ___ sprout
___ ___ stem
___ ___ trait

Name ______________________

Explore a Word

mammal—An animal with hair on its skin. A mother mammal feeds her young with milk from her body.

Follow each instruction.

1. Baby birds hatch from eggs. Tell how baby mammals are different from baby birds.

____

____

2. Fish have scales on their bodies. Tell how mammals are different from fish.

____

____

3. Draw a picture of a big mammal and a small mammal. Write the name of each mammal.

4. Write a sentence with the word *mammal*.

____

____

Name ______________________

Explore a Word

magnify—To make something seem larger.

Follow each instruction.

1. Scientists use tools to magnify things. The tools help them study things that are too small for the eyes to see clearly. Circle the names of things to magnify.

   house feather shoe ant grain of sand dog

2. Picture a bird at the top of a tall tree. Tell how someone could magnify the bird.

   ____

3. Look at the picture. Write about what is magnified.

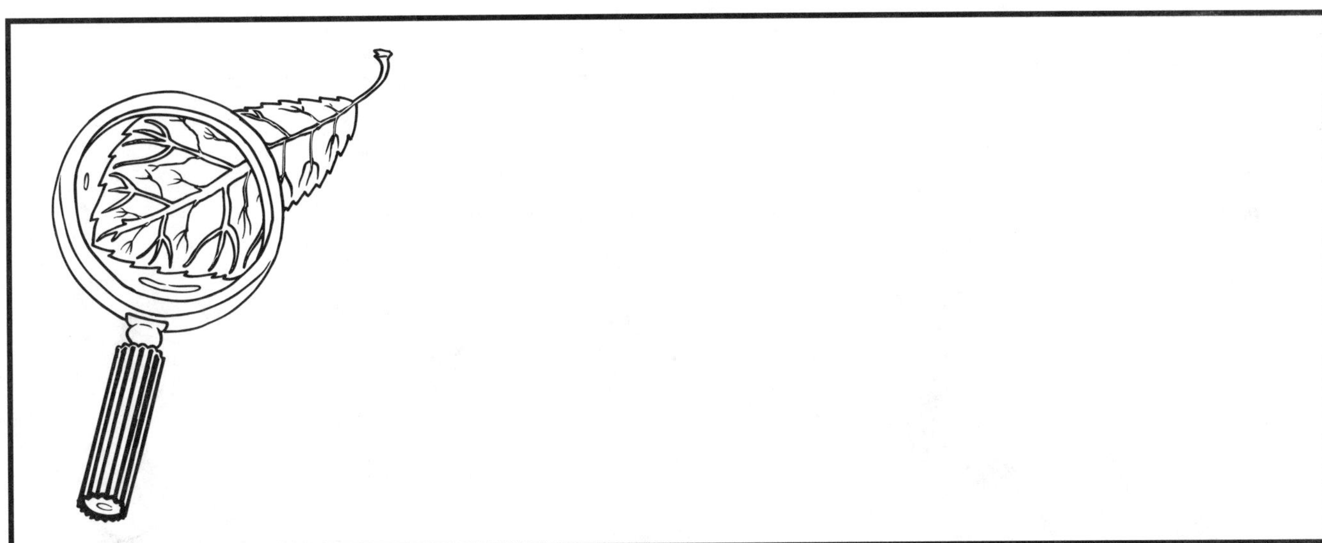

4. Write a sentence to tell what you would like to magnify and why.

   ____

   ____

Name ______________________________

Compare Words

flower—The male and female parts of a plant. The flower makes seeds that grow into new plants.

fruit—The part of a plant that holds the seeds.

Write *flower* or *fruit* on each blank.

1. The outer part of a ____________________ has colorful petals.
2. Animals eat ____________________ and drop the seeds on the ground.
3. An acorn is a ____________________ made by an oak tree.
4. A butterfly comes to a ____________________ to sip sweet nectar.
5. The seed grows inside the female part of a ____________________.
6. The wind can carry a seed inside a ____________________ to a new place.

Name ____________________

Compare Words

amphibian—An animal that has smooth skin and lives where it is wet or moist. Amphibians spend the first part of their lives in water. They get air from the water through gills.

reptile—An animal with an outer covering of scales or plates. Some reptiles live in water, but they must come up for air.

Read about each animal. Is it a reptile or an amphibian? Circle the answer.

1. A sea turtle buries its eggs on the beach.

   reptile   amphibian

2. A young frog is called a *tadpole*. It does not have legs and does not come on land.

   reptile   amphibian

3. A salamander lays its eggs in water.

   reptile   amphibian

4. Baby alligators hatch on land and head for the safety of water.

   reptile   amphibian

5. Stegosaurus was a dinosaur with bony plates on its back.

   reptile   amphibian

6. A garter snake will climb on a rock to sun itself.

   reptile   amphibian

Name ____________________

Make Connections

attract—To pull things closer.

magnetic—Able to stick to a magnet.

pole—The north or south end of a magnet.

repel—To push things away.

Complete each sentence with a vocabulary word.

1. A magnet can ____________________ paper clips made of metal.
2. A magnet will not stick to a wooden desk. Wood is not ____________________.
3. If one end of a bar magnet is labeled N, the other end must be the south ____________________.
4. The north pole of one magnet will ____________________ the north pole of another magnet.
5. Giant magnets can lift steel cars. Steel is ____________________.
6. Something that is magnetic will ____________________ a magnet.

Name ______________________

Make Connections

attract	magnetic	pole	repel

Read each sentence. Is it correct? Put a ✓ after it. If it is not correct, show how to fix it.

1. The north pole of one magnet repels the north pole of another magnet.

2. A magnet will repel something that is magnetic.

3. Pennies are made of metal, so they are magnetic.

4. Magnets attract objects made of iron.

5. A magnet shaped like a horseshoe has two south poles or two north poles.

Name ______________________________

Make Connections

constellation—A group of stars.

moon—An object in space that travels around a planet.

planet—An object in space that travels around a star.

solar system—The sun and the objects that travel around it.

Write a vocabulary word on each blank to complete the paragraph.

We live on a (1.) ______________________________ called Earth. We can see the (2.) ______________________________ that travels around the Earth. We can also see stars that make up each (3.) ______________________________ of the night sky. The stars are very far away. They are not part of our (4.) ______________________________. We do have our own star. It is called the Sun.

Name ______________________________

Make Connections

constellation	moon	planet	solar system

Read each sentence. Is it correct? Put a ✓ after it. If it is not correct, show how to fix it.

1. Jupiter and its moons are planets.

2. The Sun is at the center of our solar system.

3. A planet travels around its moon.

4. Moons form a constellation.

5. A constellation can be made of one star.

Name ______________________

Make Connections

root—The part of a plant that is underground.

seedling—A plant that has begun to grow from a seed.

soil—The tiny pieces of rock, rotting material, and living things that make up the top layer of the Earth.

sprout—To start to grow from a seed or to start to grow buds.

stem—The long main part of a plant.

Complete each sentence with a vocabulary word.

1. A ______________________ may grow into a tree if it gets enough light and water.
2. A flower forms at the top of a ______________________.
3. A plant's ______________________ holds the plant in place.
4. A ______________________ pulls in water that the plant needs.
5. Place the seed in the ground, and it may ______________________.
6. Some plants can grow in sandy ______________________.

Name ____________________

ke Connections

ne paragraph below. Think about the meaning of each **bold**

Lift your arm. You just used your **muscles**. Your muscles and the other parts of your body use **oxygen** as they work. How es your body get oxygen? You **breathe** it into your **lungs**. The ygen goes from the lungs to the **heart**. The heart is a muscle. It **mps** blood rich in oxygen throughout your body.

he vocabulary word that matches each meaning.

__________ A gas in the air.

__________ To take air into the body and send it out.

__________ Forces a gas or a liquid to move.

__________ Body parts that can squeeze, relax, and squeeze again.

__________ The body part in the chest that pumps blood.

__________ Two body parts in the chest that receive air from the mouth or nose and provide the body with oxygen.

Name ____________________

Make Connections

root	seedling	soil	sprout	stem

Read each sentence. Is it correct? Put a ✓ after it. If it is not correct, show how to fix it.

1. A plant's roots are in the stem.

2. Water travels from the stem up the roots.

3. Soil sprouts from a seedling.

4. A seedling sends roots into the soil.

5. Leaves sprout from the stem of a plant.

Name ______________________

Make Connections

Read the paragraph below. Think about the meaning of each **bold** word.

> Kittens, puppies, and the **offspring** of other mammals look like their parents. But the offspring of some animals do not have their parents' **traits** at birth. For example, a butterfly changes its form as it goes through its **life cycle**. It hatches from an egg as a **larva**, or caterpillar. It eats for weeks and grows larger and larger. Then, it turns into a **pupa** hanging inside a shell. When it finally comes out of the shell, it has the wings and body of a butterfly.

Write the vocabulary word that matches each meaning.

1. The form of an insect just after hatching. It usually looks like a worm.

   ____

2. The young of animals.

   ____

3. The changes in any living thing from its start to its adult form.

   ____

4. The stage in an insect's life when it is inside a cocoon or other case.

   ____

5. The body features and behaviors of living things.

   ____

Name ____________

Make Connections

larva	life cycle	offspring	pupa

Complete each sentence with a vocabulary word.

1. The ____________________ of a moth lies inside a c
2. An insect begins life as a ____________________.
3. An egg, a tadpole, and a frog are the stages in the ____________________ of a frog.
4. Cubs are the ____________________ of bears.
5. A ____________________ of a fly looks like a little wo
6. Hunting birds have the ____________________ of sh speed.

Name ____________________

Make Connections

breathe	heart	lungs	muscles	oxygen	pump

Complete each sentence with a vocabulary word.

1. The ____________________ in your neck allow you to turn your head.
2. Fill your ____________________ with air.
3. You cannot see ____________________ in the air, but it is all around you.
4. When you ____________________ out, you get rid of a gas called *carbon dioxide*.
5. Listen to the beats of your ____________________ inside your chest.
6. Heart muscles ____________________ blood to all parts of your body.

Name ______________________

Play With Words

Code Words

Choose the word that fits in each sentence. Circle its letter.

1. A toad is ___.
   m a mammal
   n an amphibian
   o a larva

2. A reptile breathes with ___.
   a lungs
   b traits
   c pupa

3. Scientists ___ planets to see them better.
   s constellation
   t magnify
   u magnetic

4. A seedling needs ___ to grow.
   t fruit
   u soil
   v flowers

5. The poles of two magnets may attract or ___ each other.
   r repel
   s magnetic
   t pump

6. A mammal needs ___ to stay alive.
   c offspring
   d fruit
   e oxygen

Write the circled letters in order. You will find an interesting science topic.

____

Name ______________________

Make Connections

root	seedling	soil	sprout	stem

Read each sentence. Is it correct? Put a ✓ after it. If it is not correct, show how to fix it.

1. A plant's roots are in the stem.

2. Water travels from the stem up the roots.

3. Soil sprouts from a seedling.

4. A seedling sends roots into the soil.

5. Leaves sprout from the stem of a plant.

Name ________________________

Make Connections

Read the paragraph below. Think about the meaning of each **bold** word.

Kittens, puppies, and the **offspring** of other mammals look like their parents. But the offspring of some animals do not have their parents' **traits** at birth. For example, a butterfly changes its form as it goes through its **life cycle**. It hatches from an egg as a **larva**, or caterpillar. It eats for weeks and grows larger and larger. Then, it turns into a **pupa** hanging inside a shell. When it finally comes out of the shell, it has the wings and body of a butterfly.

Write the vocabulary word that matches each meaning.

1. The form of an insect just after hatching. It usually looks like a worm.

   ____

2. The young of animals.

   ____

3. The changes in any living thing from its start to its adult form.

   ____

4. The stage in an insect's life when it is inside a cocoon or other case.

   ____

5. The body features and behaviors of living things.

   ____

Name ___________________________

Make Connections

larva	life cycle	offspring	pupa	traits

Complete each sentence with a vocabulary word.

1. The ______________________ of a moth lies inside a cocoon.
2. An insect begins life as a ______________________.
3. An egg, a tadpole, and a frog are the stages in the ______________________ of a frog.
4. Cubs are the ______________________ of bears.
5. A ______________________ of a fly looks like a little worm.
6. Hunting birds have the ______________________ of sharp eyesight and speed.

Name ______________________________

Make Connections

Read the paragraph below. Think about the meaning of each **bold** word.

Lift your arm. You just used your **muscles**. Your muscles and all the other parts of your body use **oxygen** as they work. How does your body get oxygen? You **breathe** it into your **lungs**. The oxygen goes from the lungs to the **heart**. The heart is a muscle. It **pumps** blood rich in oxygen throughout your body.

Write the vocabulary word that matches each meaning.

1. ______________________ A gas in the air.
2. ______________________ To take air into the body and send it out.
3. ______________________ Forces a gas or a liquid to move.
4. ______________________ Body parts that can squeeze, relax, and squeeze again.
5. ______________________ The body part in the chest that pumps blood.
6. ______________________ Two body parts in the chest that receive air from the mouth or nose and provide the body with oxygen.

Name ______________________________

Important Technology Words You Need to Know!

Use this list to keep track of how well you know the new words.

0 = Don't Know   1 = Know It Somewhat   2 = Know It Well

___ ___ communication
___ ___ construction
___ ___ cursor
___ ___ delete
___ ___ desktop
___ ___ file
___ ___ hardware
___ ___ insert
___ ___ manufacture
___ ___ monitor
___ ___ problem
___ ___ software
___ ___ solution
___ ___ transportation

Name ______________________________

Explore a Word

manufacture—To make things in a factory.

Follow each instruction.

1. Manufactured things are all around you. Name two manufactured things that you use.

   ____

2. Furniture is manufactured. Name two things needed to manufacture furniture.

   ____

3. Look around you. Find something that is manufactured. Find something that is NOT manufactured. Draw a picture of each one.

4. Write a sentence with the word *manufacture*.

   ____

   ____

Connections

Name ____________________

ware—The parts of a computer system.

are—The programs that run on a computer.

Information that is stored under a single name.

or—The part of a computer that has the screen.

e each sentence with a vocabulary word.

opened the ____________________ he had named "My Story."

leo game is ____________________.

mputer keyboard is ____________________.

artist used ____________________ to draw pictures.

ou want to save the changes you made to the ____________________?

at the photos on the ____________________.

Compare Words

Name ____________________

problem—Something that needs to be solved.

solution—A way to solve a problem.

Write *problem* or *solution* on each blank.

1. These heavy books are hard to carry. That is a ____________________. How can we carry heavy books? A backpack on wheels is a ____________________.

2. It used to take a long time to travel from one city to another. Cars were a great ____________________. Cars made the trips shorter. But cars use a lot of gas. That is a ____________________.

3. Water only flows down. It never flows up. How did people solve the ____________________ of getting water up from below the ground? A pump was one ____________________.

Name ______________________

Make Connections

construction—Building something.

communication—Sending and receiving messages.

transportation—Moving people and things from one place to another.

Read each sentence. Does it tell about construction, communication, or transportation? Circle the answer.

1. Two friends talk on a phone.

   construction communication transportation

2. A truck brings fresh fruit to a store.

   construction communication transportation

3. A boy reads an e-mail from his aunt far away.

   construction communication transportation

4. The house has walls made of stone.

   construction communication transportation

5. A drawing shows the plan for a tall building.

   construction communication transportation

6. Highways connect all parts of the country.

   construction communication transportation

Name _____

Make Connections

construction communication

Read each sentence. Is it correct? Put a ✓ after it.
show how to fix it.

1. Airplanes help with transportation.

2. Workers have different jobs in the communica

3. Big machines are used for the construction of

4. One form of transportation is television.

5. Freight trains are important in the construction

Make

hard

softw

file—

moni

Complet

1. Jack
2. A vid
3. A co
4. The
5. Do y

6. Look

Name ____________________

Make Connections

hardware	software	file	monitor

Read each sentence. Is it correct? Put a ✓ after it. If it is not correct, show how to fix it.

1. Photos could be in a file.

2. A computer mouse is software.

3. Click on a monitor to open it.

4. Some software helps children learn to read.

5. A computer file is hardware.

Name ______________________

Make Connections

Follow each instruction.

1. Name two forms of communication.

____

2. Name one use of software.

____

3. Name a simple kind of transportation.

____

4. Read the sentence below. Use your own words to tell what it means.

   Strong materials are needed for the construction of a bridge.

____

____

5. Use the words *problem* and *solution* in a sentence.

____

6. Make a drawing of a computer monitor. Use the word *hardware* in a sentence about your drawing.

Name ______________________

Compare Words

problem—Something that needs to be solved.

solution—A way to solve a problem.

Write *problem* or *solution* on each blank.

1. These heavy books are hard to carry. That is a ____________________. How can we carry heavy books? A backpack on wheels is a ____________________.

2. It used to take a long time to travel from one city to another. Cars were a great ____________________. Cars made the trips shorter. But cars use a lot of gas. That is a ____________________.

3. Water only flows down. It never flows up. How did people solve the ____________________ of getting water up from below the ground? A pump was one ____________________.

Name ___________________________

Make Connections

construction—Building something.

communication—Sending and receiving messages.

transportation—Moving people and things from one place to another.

Read each sentence. Does it tell about construction, communication, or transportation? Circle the answer.

1. Two friends talk on a phone.

   construction communication transportation

2. A truck brings fresh fruit to a store.

   construction communication transportation

3. A boy reads an e-mail from his aunt far away.

   construction communication transportation

4. The house has walls made of stone.

   construction communication transportation

5. A drawing shows the plan for a tall building.

   construction communication transportation

6. Highways connect all parts of the country.

   construction communication transportation

Name ______________________

Make Connections

construction	communication	transportation

Read each sentence. Is it correct? Put a ✓ after it. If it is not correct, show how to fix it.

1. Airplanes help with transportation.

2. Workers have different jobs in the communication of a building.

3. Big machines are used for the construction of a road.

4. One form of transportation is television.

5. Freight trains are important in the construction of food.

Name ______________________

Make Connections

hardware—The parts of a computer system.

software—The programs that run on a computer.

file—Information that is stored under a single name.

monitor—The part of a computer that has the screen.

Complete each sentence with a vocabulary word.

1. Jack opened the ____________________ he had named "My Story."
2. A video game is ____________________.
3. A computer keyboard is ____________________.
4. The artist used ____________________ to draw pictures.
5. Do you want to save the changes you made to the ____________________?
6. Look at the photos on the ____________________.

Name ______________________

Make Connections

hardware	software	file	monitor

Read each sentence. Is it correct? Put a ✓ after it. If it is not correct, show how to fix it.

1. Photos could be in a file.

2. A computer mouse is software.

3. Click on a monitor to open it.

4. Some software helps children learn to read.

5. A computer file is hardware.

Name ______________________

Make Connections

Read the paragraph below. Think about the meaning of each **bold** word.

Use the mouse to click on a file on the **desktop**. Use keys or the mouse to **scroll** down the pages. Place the **cursor** where you want to work. You might **insert** new text. Or, you might **delete** text that is there.

Write the vocabulary word that matches each meaning.

1. The display of a background and small pictures of programs and files.

   ____

2. The blinking bar that marks the place to type.

   ____

3. To get rid of text or pictures.

   ____

4. To make text and pictures move up, down, left, or right on a computer screen.

   ____

5. To add text or pictures.

   ____

Name ____________________

Make Connections

cursor	desktop	insert	scroll	delete

Complete each sentence with a vocabulary word.

1. The ____________________ goes dark to use less energy.
2. You can ____________________ a word and insert a better one.
3. The ____________________ moves as you type.
4. Please ____________________ a period at the end of the sentence.
5. One way to ____________________ is with the Page Up and Page Down keys.
6. The ____________________ blinks on a point in the text.

Name ______________________

Make Connections

Follow each instruction.

1. Name two forms of communication.

____

2. Name one use of software.

____

3. Name a simple kind of transportation.

____

4. Read the sentence below. Use your own words to tell what it means.

   Strong materials are needed for the construction of a bridge.

____

____

5. Use the words *problem* and *solution* in a sentence.

____

6. Make a drawing of a computer monitor. Use the word *hardware* in a sentence about your drawing.

Name ________________________

Play With Words

Code Words

Choose the word that fits in each sentence. Circle its letter.

1. Buses, trucks, and jets are kinds of ___.
   - **j** software
   - **k** communication
   - **l** transportation

2. The cursor shows where to ___ text.
   - **a** insert
   - **b** file
   - **c** desktop

3. Steel is used in the ___ of buildings.
   - **o** monitor
   - **p** construction
   - **q** solution

4. Letters and e-mail are written ___.
   - **t** communication
   - **u** hardware
   - **v** delete

5. Machines are built to solve ___.
   - **m** solutions
   - **n** manufacture
   - **o** problems

6. Use the ___ key to get rid of text.
   - **l** cursor
   - **m** scroll
   - **p** delete

Write the circled letters in order. You will find the name of a kind of computer.

____

Name ______________________

Play With Words

Vocabulary Search

Read each meaning. Which vocabulary word matches that meaning? Write it on the line. Then, find the word in the puzzle. The words go across and down.

1. To build or make something ______________________
2. The parts of a computer ______________________
3. Computer programs ______________________
4. The end of a problem ______________________
5. To erase on a computer ______________________
6. The display on a monitor ______________________

E	D	U	B	D	E	S	K	T	O	P	A
F	A	N	I	T	H	X	O	Y	D	L	G
L	P	C	Q	G	K	E	T	S	M	I	D
U	O	S	O	L	U	T	I	O	N	W	E
I	S	H	E	D	A	L	C	F	B	F	L
S	M	A	N	U	F	A	C	T	U	R	E
C	H	R	V	G	O	P	N	W	J	O	T
E	M	D	R	F	I	N	L	A	A	Y	E
G	V	W	B	A	T	U	W	R	T	C	S
D	J	A	L	H	E	I	O	E	N	Z	D
A	Z	R	O	Y	K	N	P	S	W	G	R
M	C	E	X	I	F	B	U	L	E	H	O

Name ___________________

Important Language Arts Words You Need to Know!

Use this list to keep track of how well you know the new words.

0 = Don't Know　　　I = Know It Somewhat　　　2 = Know It Well

___ ___ alphabetical order
___ ___ author
___ ___ capitalize
___ ___ cause-effect
___ ___ chapter
___ ___ character
___ ___ compound word
___ ___ consonant
___ ___ contraction
___ ___ description
___ ___ detail
___ ___ exclamation point
___ ___ heading
___ ___ illustrator
___ ___ main idea
___ ___ paragraph
___ ___ period
___ ___ phonics
___ ___ play
___ ___ poem
___ ___ prediction
___ ___ question mark
___ ___ rhyme
___ ___ sentence
___ ___ setting
___ ___ strategy
___ ___ summary
___ ___ syllable
___ ___ table of contents
___ ___ vowel

Name ____________________

Explore a Word

description—Words that tell about what something is like.

Follow each instruction.

1. A description tells what something looks like. Write five describing words to tell about color, size, and shape.

____

2. A description can tell about other senses. Write words to describe a sound, a touch, a taste, and a smell.

____

____

3. Think of your favorite food. Draw a picture of the food. Write words that give a clear description of it.

4. Write a sentence with the word *description*.

____

Name ______________________

Explore a Word

cause-effect—A cause is what makes something happen. An effect is what happens.

Follow each instruction.

1. What might cause a fire? What could be an effect of a fire? Write a cause and an effect.

   cause: ______________________

   effect: ______________________

2. Read the sentences below. Label the cause and the effect.

   Allie's belly hurts. She ate too much ice cream!

3. Look at the picture. Write about the cause and effect.

4. Write a sentence with *because* in the middle. Then, write *cause* and *effect* to label the parts of the sentence.

____

____

Name ______________________

Compare Words

author—Someone who writes a story or a book.

illustrator—Someone who draws pictures for a story or a book.

Write *author* or *illustrator* on each blank.

1. The ____________________ made funny drawings.
2. The writer of a picture book may also be the ____________________.
3. Emily read two books written by the same ____________________.
4. The ____________________ came up with an idea for a story.
5. An ____________________ has studied art in school.
6. This book has no pictures. Who is its ____________________?

Name ______________________

Compare Words

compound word—A word made of two smaller words.

contraction—A word made by shortening two words. An apostrophe (') stands for one or more missing letters.

Read each word in the box. What are the two words in it? Write both words in the chart.

don't	we're	you're	wouldn't	they've
cannot	somewhere	yourself	firewood	thunderstorm

Compound Words	Contractions
______________	______________
______________	______________
______________	______________
______________	______________
______________	______________

Name ____________________

Make Connections

chapter—A section of a book.

play—A story for actors.

poem—A piece of writing set out in lines.

rhyme—The same ending sounds.

table of contents—A list of the chapters in a book.

Complete each sentence with a vocabulary word.

1. Use the ____________________ to find Chapter 4.
2. The words *head* and *red* ____________________.
3. Watch a ____________________ on a stage.
4. Listen to the rhymes as I read aloud this ____________________.
5. Adam has the role of the lion in the ____________________.
6. Each ____________________ of the book begins on a new page.

Name ____________________

Make Connections

chapter	play	poem	rhyme	table of contents

Read each sentence. Is it correct? Put a ✓ after it. If it is not correct, show how to fix it.

1. We wore masks to perform our table of contents.

2. The words *fast* and *fats* rhyme.

3. A play has chapters.

4. A chapter lists the poems in a book.

5. A poem may have rhyme.

Name ______________________

Make Connections

alphabetical order—ABC order.

consonant—A letter or a sound that is not a vowel.

phonics—Letters and their sounds.

syllable—A word or part of a word with only one vowel sound.

vowel—The letters *a*, *e*, *i*, *o*, *u* and their sounds.

Circle the answer to each question

1. Which word has the same vowel sound as in *leaf*?

   loaf life keep

2. Which list of names is in alphabetical order?

   Rob, Fred, Elly Elly, Fred, Rob Elly, Rob, Fred

3. Which word begins and ends with a consonant sound?

   toe time aim

4. Which word has one syllable?

   screamed person navy

5. Which sentence tells about phonics?

   The word *cup* means "something to drink from."
   The word *cup* is like *glass* and *mug*.
   The word *cup* begins with a *c* that sounds like *k*.

6. Which word has two consonants and one vowel?

   ape fat step

Name ______________________

Make Connections

alphabetical order	consonant	phonics	syllable	vowel

Read each sentence. Is it correct? Put a ✓ after it. If it is not correct, show how to fix it.

1. Use phonics to put the name *James* before the name *Pam*.

2. The word *happy* has one syllable.

3. There are three vowels in the word *bump*.

4. A syllable has one vowel sound.

5. Put your lips together and hum to make a vowel sound.

Name ____________________

Make Connections

capitalize—To begin a word with an uppercase, or capital, letter.

exclamation point—The end mark (!) that shows excitement.

period—The end mark (.) that shows the end of a sentence.

question mark—The end mark (?) that shows a question.

sentence—A group of words that shows a complete thought.

Complete each sentence with a vocabulary word.

1. A question is a kind of ____________________.
2. Put an ____________________ after a word like *Wow*.
3. Most sentences have a ____________________ at the end.
4. You should ____________________ the first word of a sentence.
5. If you write an asking sentence, put a ____________________ at the end.
6. Be sure to ____________________ the name of your city or town.

Name ______________________________

Make Connections

capitalize	exclamation point	period	question mark	sentence

Fix each sentence. Circle the reason why you corrected it.

1. Today was the best day ever — capitalize — exclamation point
2. My friend eddie has a dog. — capitalize — period
3. We all should — sentence — exclamation point
4. Can we go — period — question mark
5. The cat slept — sentence — period

Name ______________________________

Make Connections

Read the paragraph below. Think about the meaning of each **bold** word.

The main **character** in this story is a boy who is looking for a lost dog. The **setting** is the boy's neighborhood on a Sunday afternoon. Readers look for clues about where the boy will hunt next. The **strategy** of making **predictions** helps readers keep track of the events in the story.

Write the vocabulary word that matches each meaning.

1. ________________________ Where and when a story takes place.
2. ________________________ Good guesses about what will happen next.
3. ________________________ Steps to take to read with understanding.
4. ________________________ A person or an animal in a story.

Name ______________________

Make Connections

character	prediction	setting	strategy

Complete each sentence with a vocabulary word.

1. The ____________________ of this story is a forest at night.
2. Each ____________________ talks in a story.
3. As you read, ask yourself, "Do I understand?" Asking questions is a good ____________________.
4. It can be fun to make a ____________________ about how a story will end.
5. The main ____________________ in this story is a sly fox.
6. Making predictions is a ____________________ that helps you think about what you are reading.

Name ______________________

Make Connections

Read the paragraph below. Think about the meaning of each **bold** word.

When you read information, look at the **heading** above each section. Each **paragraph** has a **main idea**. Each paragraph also has **details** that tell more about the main idea. Think about the headings and the main ideas. Then, you can make a **summary** of the information.

Write the vocabulary word that matches each meaning.

1. ______________________ A group of sentences about one main idea.
2. ______________________ The most important idea about a topic.
3. ______________________ A title for a section of information.
4. ______________________ Pieces of information in a paragraph.
5. ______________________ A shortened form of a story. It gives only the most important ideas and information.

Name ______________________________

Make Connections

detail	heading	main idea	paragraph	summary

Complete each sentence with a vocabulary word.

1. The ________________________ of a paragraph could be in the first sentence.
2. Do not include many details in your ________________________.
3. Get ready to understand an article by reading each ________________________ above a section.
4. A ________________________ has a main idea and details.
5. The answer to the question *Who?* is a ________________________ of information.
6. The first sentence of a ________________________ begins on a new line.

Name ____________________

Play With Words

Code Words

Choose the word that fits in each sentence. Circle its letter.

1. A chapter has ___ in it.
   m illustrators
   n paragraphs
   o alphabetical order

2. The word *sentence* has two ___.
   e syllables
   f periods
   g consonants

3. The words *you're* and *you'll* are ___.
   c capitalized
   d compound words
   e contractions

4. An asking sentence ends with ___.
   d a question mark
   e a period
   f an exclamation point

5. Make a ___ about what will happen next in the story.
   k description
   l prediction
   m summary

6. You may hear ___ in a poem.
   d strategies
   e rhyme
   f alphabetical order

Write the circled letters in order. You will find the answer to this riddle: *What has an eye that never shuts?*

____

Name ____________________

Important History Words You Need to Know!

Use this list to keep track of how well you know the new words.

0 = Don't Know 1 = Know It Somewhat 2 = Know It Well

___ ___ celebration
___ ___ colony
___ ___ community
___ ___ event
___ ___ future
___ ___ heroism
___ ___ legend
___ ___ liberty
___ ___ modern
___ ___ nation
___ ___ past
___ ___ present
___ ___ symbol
___ ___ Thanksgiving
___ ___ timeline

Name ____________________

Explore a Word

symbol—A picture or thing that stands for an idea.

Follow each instruction.

1. A flag is a symbol. Describe a flag. Tell what it stands for.

____

____

2. Look at a coin or a bill of paper money. Name a symbol you see. Tell what you think it stands for.

____

____

3. Draw a picture of another symbol you have seen. Write to tell what it is and what it stands for.

4. Write a sentence with the word *symbol*.

____

____

Name ______________________

Explore a Word

legend—A story first told long ago.

Follow each instruction.

1. A legend may be based on real people from long ago. For example, many legends are told about George Washington. Tell how a legend about George Washington is different from a book of information about him.

____

____

2. A legend and a fairy-tale are both old stories. Name one difference between a legend and a fairy-tale.

____

____

3. Look at the picture. Write a sentence to tell about the book.

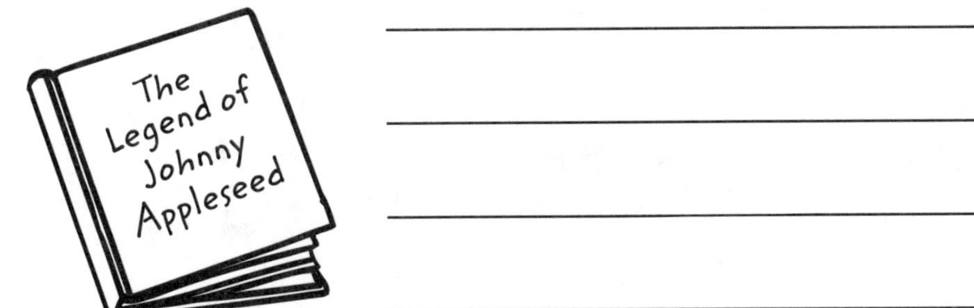

____

____

____

____

4. Write a sentence with the word *legend*.

____

____

Name ____________________

Compare Words

past—Times that have gone by.

present—Times we are living in.

Each sentence tells about the place where you live. Does it tell about the past or the present? Circle the answer.

1. People use horses to travel from one town to another.

   past present

2. People get meat by hunting wild animals.

   past present

3. People buy food in supermarkets.

   past present

4. Travelers drive cars to the nearest airport.

   past present

5. Young children work on farms or in factories.

   past present

6. People use computers to get information.

   past present

Name ___________________

Make Connections

event—Something that happens.

future—Times that have not happened yet.

modern—Of the present time.

timeline—A line that shows events in order of time.

Complete each sentence with a vocabulary word.

1. Nobody knows what will happen in the _______________.
2. The _______________ shows the years 1850 through 1860.
3. We live in _______________ times.
4. The present comes between the past and the _______________.
5. The battle was a famous _______________ in history.
6. Make a _______________ of the important events in your life.

Name ______________________

Make Connections

event	future	modern	timeline

Read each sentence. Is it correct? Put a ✓ after it. If it is not correct, show how to fix it.

1. A modern house looks old.

2. Important events have happened in the future.

3. The year 1900 comes after 1890 on a timeline.

4. An event could be surprising.

5. A timeline shows future events.

Name ______________________

Make Connections

heroism—The actions of a hero, or brave person.

liberty—Freedom.

nation—A country.

Complete each sentence with a vocabulary word.

1. The United States is a ______________________.

2. People want the ______________________ to live where they want.

3. The soldier received a medal for ______________________.

4. People show ______________________ when they risk their lives to help others.

5. Every ______________________ has its own flag.

6. We can speak and act freely because we have ______________________.

Name ______________________________

Make Connections

nation	liberty	heroism

Read each sentence. Is it correct? Put a ✓ after it. If it is not correct, show how to fix it.

1. An act of heroism is an everyday event.

2. Africa is a nation.

3. A nation may fight for liberty.

4. Canada and Mexico are nations.

5. The Statue of Heroism welcomes people to the United States.

Name ____________________

Make Connections

Read the paragraph below. Think about the meaning of each **bold** word.

In almost every **community** in the United States, families gather for a **celebration** in November. It is the holiday of **Thanksgiving**. Americans remember the little **colony** of English people in Massachusetts and the feast they held in the fall of 1621.

Write the vocabulary word that matches each meaning.

1. ____________________ A day of feasting and giving thanks throughout the nation.

2. ____________________ A group of people from one land who live and work together in a new land.

3. ____________________ A group of people who live in the same area.

4. ____________________ A way to remember a special and happy event.

Name ____________________

Make Connections

celebration	colony	community	Thanksgiving

Read each sentence. Is it correct? Put a ✓ after it. If it is not correct, show how to fix it.

1. The best-known Thanksgiving food is spaghetti.

2. A celebration is a sad event.

3. A big city has many colonies.

4. After the United States became a nation, it was made of thirteen colonies.

5. A colony is a community of people from another land.

Name ______________________

Make Connections

Follow each instruction.

1. Name a symbol of Thanksgiving.

____

2. Describe something seen at a celebration.

____

3. Name three nations.

____

4. Read the sentence below. Use your own words to tell what it means.

   The American colonies fought for liberty from Britain.

____

____

5. Use the words *legend* and *heroism* in a sentence.

____

____

6. Make a drawing to show your idea about the words *past*, *present*, and *future*.

Name ______________________

Play With Words

Code Words

Choose the word that fits in each sentence. Circle its letter.

1. A ___ shows dates and events.
   - **k** celebration
   - **l** symbol
   - **m** timeline

2. The ___ comes after the present.
   - **u** future
   - **v** modern
   - **w** past

3. The first airplane flight was an important ___.
   - **r** symbol
   - **s** event
   - **t** legend

4. We are all part of a ___.
   - **e** community
   - **f** colony
   - **g** timeline

5. We use ___ machines.
   - **s** timeline
   - **t** future
   - **u** modern

6. The colonies won their ___ and became a nation.
   - **k** heroism
   - **l** celebration
   - **m** liberty

Write the circled letters in order. You will find a place to learn about history.

____

Name ______________________

Important Geography Words You Need to Know!

Use this list to keep track of how well you know the new words.

0 = Don't Know   1 = Know It Somewhat   2 = Know It Well

___ ___ bay
___ ___ coast
___ ___ direction
___ ___ east
___ ___ globe
___ ___ grid
___ ___ island
___ ___ legend
___ ___ location
___ ___ north
___ ___ northeast
___ ___ northwest
___ ___ ocean
___ ___ route
___ ___ rural
___ ___ south
___ ___ southeast
___ ___ southwest
___ ___ urban
___ ___ west

Name ______________________

Explore a Word

globe—The Earth shown on a ball.

Follow each instruction.

1. Name two ways that a globe is like the real Earth.

____

____

2. Tell what you would use a globe for.

____

____

3. Look at the picture. Add labels to tell about what is shown.

4. Read the sentence below. Use your own words to tell what it means.

The travelers visited cities throughout the globe.

____

____

Name ___________________________

Explore a Word

location—Where on the Earth a place is found.

Follow each instruction.

1. When you locate something, you find its *location*. Name two ways to find a location.

____

____

2. Name the location of your school.

____

____

3. Look at the map. Find the four corners where Fifth Street and Montrose Avenue meet. Draw a star to show that location.

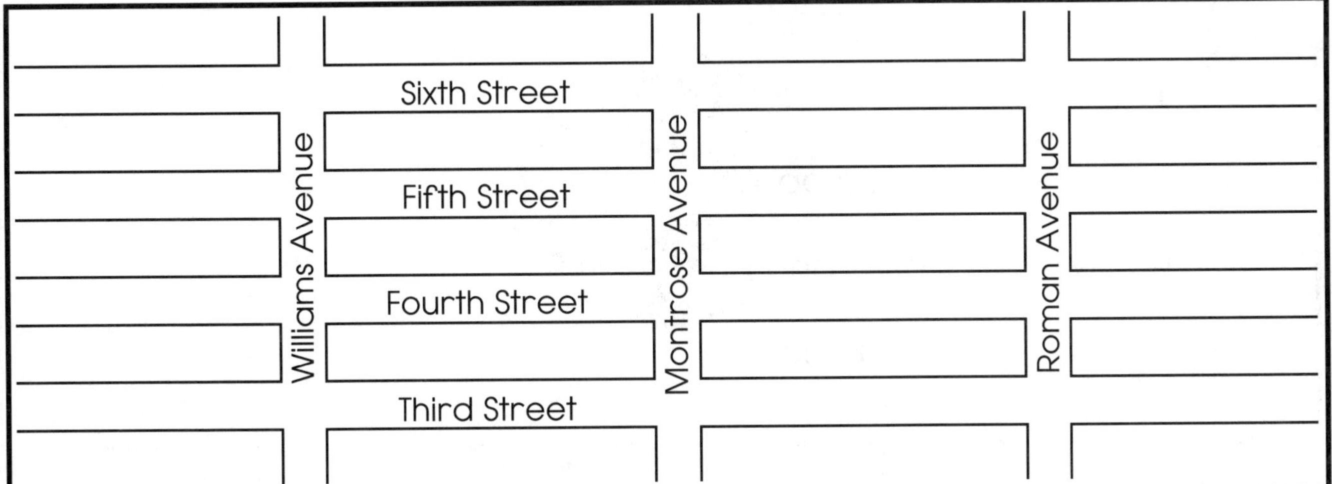

4. Write a sentence with the word *location*.

____

____

Name ______________________

Compare Words

rural—Having to do with country life.

urban—Having to do with city life.

Read about each place. Is it rural or urban? Circle the answer.

1. Cows are eating grass in a field.

   rural   urban

2. A road passes through a forest.

   rural   urban

3. Cars, trucks, and buses fill the streets.

   rural   urban

4. People live in apartment buildings.

   rural   urban

5. Corn is growing everywhere you look.

   rural   urban

6. There are many stores and businesses.

   rural   urban

Name ______________________

Make Connections

grid—Lines that cross a map to help readers find a location.

legend—The key to the symbols on a map.

route—The path from one location to another.

Complete each sentence with a vocabulary word.

1. This bus takes a ______________________ down Third Avenue.

2. A map of the city has green squares on it. The ______________________ shows that a green square stands for a park.

3. The picture below shows a ______________________.

	1	2	3	4
A				
B				
C				
D				

4. We marked the road map to show the ______________________ we would take from Texas to California.

5. A map ______________________ is like a list of pictures and their meanings.

6. Look for Florence Street at E–10 on the ______________________ of the map.

Name ______________________

Make Connections

grid	legend	route

Read each sentence. Is it correct? Put a ✓ after it. If it is not correct, show how to fix it.

1. A map legend is an old story.

2. A route is a straight line.

3. The grid on a map forms squares.

4. Look at the route to understand the symbols on a map.

5. What is your grid from home to school?

Name ______________________

Make Connections

direction—The way in which something moves or points.

east—Toward the right side of a world map.

west—Toward the left side of a world map.

north—Toward the top of a world map.

south—Toward the bottom of a world map.

Complete each sentence with a vocabulary word.

1. The sun seems to rise in the east and set in the ______________________.
2. Run your finger ______________________ to the top of a globe.
3. In which ______________________ should we travel to reach Mexico?
4. If I point left to show north, then ______________________ is to my right.
5. Most states are ______________________ of California.
6. Walk north, and then turn right to go ______________________.

Name ______________________

Make Connections

direction	east	west	north	south

Read each sentence. Is it correct? Put a ✓ after it. If it is not correct, show how to fix it.

1. The four main directions are north, south, east, and west.

2. Run your finger down a map of the world to go north.

3. If you are facing east, the direction south is behind you.

4. Canada is west of the United States.

5. In this picture, one arrow points to a question mark. That direction is west.

Name ____________________

Make Connections

northeast—In a direction between north and east.

southeast—In a direction between south and east.

northwest—In a direction between north and west.

southwest—In a direction between south and west.

This map shows the state of Tennessee. Look at the map to circle the answer to each question.

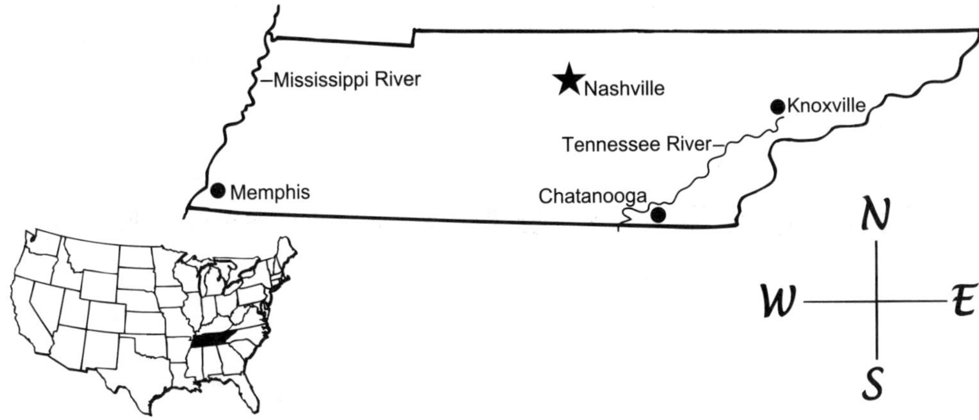

1. The state of Tennessee is in the ____________________ of the United States.

   northwest   southeast   southwest

2. The capital city of Nashville is ____________________ of Memphis.

   northwest   southeast   southwest

3. Start at Knoxville, and travel ____________________ to reach Chattanooga.

   northwest   southeast   southwest

4. Start at Chattanooga, and travel ____________________ to reach Nashville.

   northwest   southeast   southwest

Name ______________________

Make Connections

northeast	southeast	northwest	southwest

Read each sentence. Is it correct? Put a ✓ after it. If it is not correct, show how to fix it.

1. The direction northwest is halfway between north and east.

2. If you are facing northeast, the direction southwest is behind you.

3. The state of Florida is in the northwest of the United States.

4. The direction northeast is toward the left and bottom of a world map.

5. In this picture, one arrow points to a question mark. That direction is southwest.

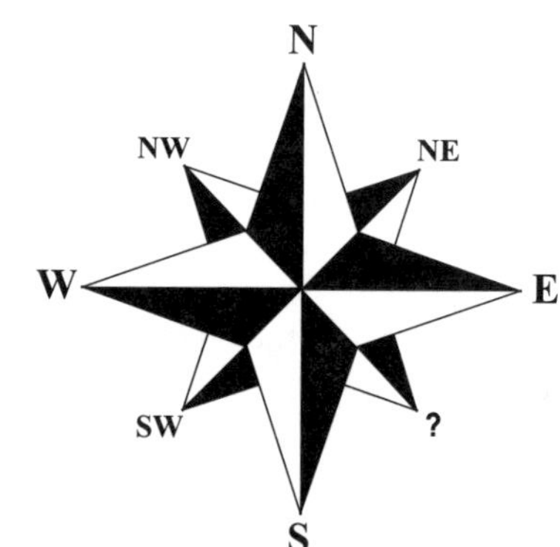

Name ______________________

Make Connections

bay—A part of the sea that reaches a wide curve of shore.

coast—Land that meets the sea.

island—Land surrounded by water.

ocean—Any of the largest bodies of salt water on the Earth.

Complete each sentence with a vocabulary word.

1. The ______________________ is also called the *sea*.
2. People on the ______________________ take a ferry to reach the mainland.
3. The name of one ______________________ is the Atlantic.
4. Boats sail into the ______________________, where the water is calmer.
5. People who live along a ______________________ may enjoy going to a beach.
6. A small, rocky ______________________ lies off the shore.

Name ____________________

Make Connections

bay	coast	island	ocean

Read each sentence. Is it correct? Put a ✓ after it. If it is not correct, show how to fix it.

1. A bay is surrounded by water.

2. Islands are found only in the ocean.

3. The ocean coast is the same as the seashore.

4. A bay could have an island in it.

5. A bay is far from a coast.

Name ____________________

Make Connections

Follow each instruction.

1. Name one difference between a map and a globe.

2. Write the word that matches each direction shown.

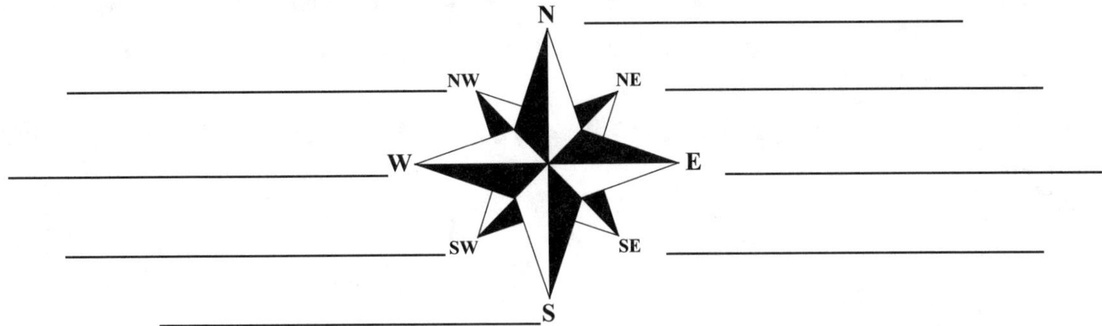

3. Draw two pictures to show the difference between *urban* and *rural*. Use those words to label the pictures.

4. Read the list of words. Cross out the word that does not belong with the others. Tell why it does not belong.

legend   ocean   bay   coast

____

5. Use the words *route* and *location* in a sentence.

____

____

Name ______________________

Play With Words

Code Words

Choose the word that fits in each sentence. Circle its letter.

1. Travel in a southeast ___.
   f northwest
   g direction
   h rural

2. A ___ may cover a map.
   l grid
   m legend
   n location

3. Water surrounds the ___.
   m legend
   n bay
   o island

4. Too much traffic is one ___ problem.
   a rural
   b urban
   c ocea

5. Every ocean beach is along a ___.
   a coast
   b grid
   c ba

6. Mark a ___ on a map.
   j globe
   k southwest
   l route

Write the circled letters in order. You will find a word that means *"all over the world."*

____

Name ______________________________

Important Civics and Economics Words You Need to Know!

Use this list to keep track of how well you know the new words.

0 = Don't Know   1 = Know It Somewhat   2 = Know It Well

___ ___ buyer
___ ___ citizen
___ ___ elect
___ ___ election
___ ___ goods
___ ___ govern
___ ___ government
___ ___ governor
___ ___ honesty
___ ___ justice
___ ___ law
___ ___ mayor
___ ___ needs
___ ___ president
___ ___ price
___ ___ purchase
___ ___ product
___ ___ responsibility
___ ___ rights
___ ___ seller
___ ___ service
___ ___ state
___ ___ tax
___ ___ vote
___ ___ wants

Name ______________________

Explore a Word

honesty—Telling the truth.

Follow each instruction.

1. You can trust a person who has honesty. Tell why.

____

____

2. Anna borrowed her friend's doll. She left the doll outside. When she went outside, it was gone. What should Anna say to show honesty?

____

____

3. Look at the pictures. Label one picture with the word *honesty*. Label the other picture with a word that means the opposite of *honesty*.

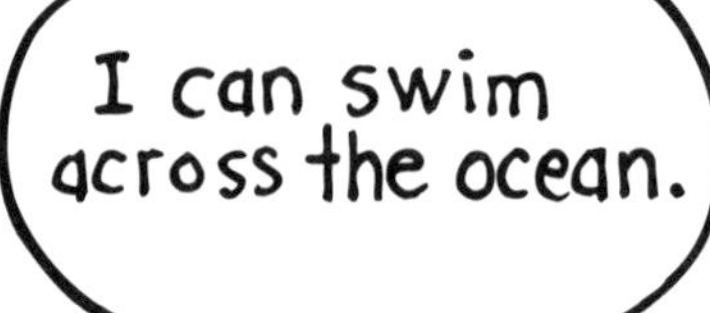

4. Read the sentence below. Use your own words to tell what it means.

Sometimes, it is hard to show honesty.

____

____

Name ______________________

Explore a Word

justice—Fair treatment for everyone.

Follow each instruction.

1. Do you want a teacher to show justice? Tell why you think that.

____

____

2. Name one reason that a person might want justice.

____

____

3. Look at the picture. It shows a symbol of justice. Tell why it is a good symbol.

4. Read the sentences below. Replace each underlined word with *fair* or *fairness*.

We act in a <u>just</u> way. We believe in <u>justice</u> for all.

Name ______________________

Compare Words

needs—Things that people must have to live.

wants—Things that people would like to have.

Read the name of each thing. Is it a need or a want? Circle the answer.

1. fresh water for drinking

   need want

2. the newest video game

   need want

3. warm clothing for a cold winter

   need want

4. chips and other snacks

   need want

5. enough food for daily meals

   need want

6. a house or other place to live

   need want

Name ____________________

Compare Words

goods—Things for sale.

services—Work that people do for others.

Read each sentence. Does it tell about goods or a service? Circle the answer.

1. My dentist cleaned my teeth.

   goods service

2. I bought a gallon of milk.

   goods service

3. I got a haircut at Bo's Barbershop.

   goods service

4. I love the fresh rolls at the bakery.

   goods service

5. How much did my sneakers cost?

   goods service

6. Ms. Wilson taught me to read.

   goods service

Name ______________________

Compare Words

right—The freedom to do something.

responsibility—An action that someone must take.

Write *right* or *responsibility* on each blank.

1. Students have the ____________________ to go to school. It is their ____________________ to try their best to learn.

2. Americans have the ____________________ to live where they wish. They have the ____________________ to be good neighbors.

3. Every child has the ____________________ to follow the rules on the playground. If children do not behave safely, their ____________________ to use the public playground could be taken away.

Name ______________________

Make Connections

citizen—A person born in a country or a person who becomes a member of that country.

elect—To pick someone by voting.

election—The event at which people vote for someone.

law—A rule that everyone must follow.

vote—To make a choice.

Complete each sentence with a vocabulary word.

1. Every grown-up ____________________ has the right to vote.

2. Americans will choose their leaders in the next ____________________.

3. Stop at a red traffic light. That is the ____________________!

4. Our class will ____________________ to pick a place for a field trip.

5. Citizens ____________________ the people who will pass laws.

6. Sometimes, we raise our hands to ____________________ for something.

Name ______________________

Make Connections

citizen	elect	election	laws	vote

Read each sentence. Is it correct? Put a ✓ after it. If it is not correct, show how to fix it.

1. Someone might vote by marking a piece of paper.

2. All American citizens have the right to elect.

3. People may vote about laws.

4. We counted the laws to see who won the election.

5. People voted in the last citizen.

Name ______________________

Make Connections

Read the paragraphs below. Think about the meaning of each **bold** word.

Voters in our city have elected Linda Feng as our new **mayor**. Feng has said, "Citizens must trust their **government**. And I promise to **govern** wisely and fairly."

Citizens will soon vote for the next **governor** of our **state**. The **president** plans to visit our state to tell voters to re-elect Governor Brown.

Write the vocabulary word that matches each meaning.

1. ______________________ To lead a city, state, or country.
2. ______________________ A group that makes laws and sees that they are obeyed.
3. ______________________ The leader of a state's government.
4. ______________________ The leader of a city's government.
5. ______________________ The leader of a country's government.
6. ______________________ An area that makes up part of a country and has its own government.

Name ______________________

Make Connections

govern	government	governor	mayor	president	state

Read each sentence. Is it correct? Put a ✓ after it. If it is not correct, show how to fix it.

1. The leader of a state is a mayor.

2. The leader of a country is a governor.

3. Voters elect the people who will govern them.

4. There are fifty mayors in the United States.

5. The governor of the United States is based in Washington, D.C.

6. The president is the head of the United States government.

Name ______________________

Make Connections

buyer—Someone who buys something with money.

price—How much money is paid for something.

product—A thing that is made for sale.

purchase—To pay money for.

seller—A person or store with something for sale.

tax—Money paid to the government.

Complete each sentence with a vocabulary word.

1. My sister paid a high ______________ for new shoes.
2. The state government collects a sales ______________.
3. Mal's Sports Shop is a ______________ of hockey skates.
4. What would you ______________ with $100?
5. Mom is looking for a ______________ who wants a used bike.
6. A car, a banana, or a chair is a ______________ that people buy and sell.

Name ____________________

Make Connections

buyer	price	product	purchase	seller	tax

Read each sentence. Is it correct? Put a ✓ after it. If it is not correct, show how to fix it.

1. Workers pay a product to the government.

2. The tax of this carton of juice is $2.50.

3. A factory could make a product.

4. If you purchase a product, you are a seller.

5. Most sellers like lower prices.

6. A seller and a buyer could agree on a price for a product.

Name ____________________

Play With Words

Code Words

Choose the word that fits in each sentence. Circle its letter.

1. We want honesty and ___.
   - **l** election
   - **m** taxes
   - **n** justice

2. Buyers ___ goods and services.
   - **a** purchase
   - **b** sellers
   - **c** product

3. A ___ leads a state.
   - **t** governor
   - **u** mayor
   - **v** citizen

4. Voting is a citizen's ___.
   - **h** government
   - **i** responsibility
   - **j** president

5. Doctors and teachers give ___.
   - **m** goods
   - **n** products
   - **o** services

6. Everyone has wants and ___.
   - **l** prices
   - **m** taxes
   - **n** needs

Write the circled letters in order. You will find a word that completes the sentence below.

The president governs the ____________________.

Name ______________________

Play With Words

Vocabulary Search

Read each meaning. Which vocabulary word matches that meaning? Write it on the line. Then, find the word in the puzzle. The words go across and down.

1. The leader of a city ______________________
2. Fairness ______________________
3. The leader of the United States ______________________
4. The people who make laws ______________________
5. An event for voters ______________________
6. Products made for sale ______________________

P	R	E	S	I	D	E	N	T	A	I	B
E	D	J	C	H	L	M	U	F	J	E	G
Q	F	O	R	A	B	I	T	V	U	N	S
E	L	I	T	G	U	S	H	M	S	K	D
G	O	V	E	R	N	M	E	N	T	B	T
O	F	D	A	H	K	A	O	L	I	N	F
O	S	B	M	G	I	Y	C	J	C	E	R
D	A	L	Q	O	S	O	D	U	E	X	V
S	R	V	N	R	H	R	F	W	Y	I	Z
M	C	D	E	G	O	T	S	L	E	W	M
I	K	A	J	E	L	E	C	T	I	O	N
E	G	N	C	U	L	B	D	I	O	H	A

Name ____________________

Important Art Words You Need to Know!

Use this list to keep track of how well you know the new words.

0 = Don't Know   1 = Know It Somewhat   2 = Know It Well

___ ___ actor
___ ___ balance
___ ___ band
___ ___ cast
___ ___ colorful
___ ___ compose
___ ___ costume
___ ___ dancer
___ ___ director
___ ___ guitar
___ ___ instrument
___ ___ musician
___ ___ note
___ ___ pattern
___ ___ pluck
___ ___ pottery
___ ___ realistic
___ ___ rehearse
___ ___ scenery
___ ___ sculpture
___ ___ solo
___ ___ stage
___ ___ stretch
___ ___ strum
___ ___ twirl

Name ______________________

Explore a Word

pattern—Lines, colors, or shapes that repeat to make a design.

Follow each instruction.

1. A shirt may have a pattern of stripes on it. Name another pattern that you can see on clothing.

   ____

2. Circle the things that have patterns.

   wallpaper   snowflakes   blue sky   a rug   a glass of milk

3. Draw a pattern using lines and dots. Write a few words to describe the pattern.

4. Complete the sentence below with your own idea.

   People like to look at patterns because ______________________

   ____

Name ______________________

Explore a Word

realistic—In a way that seems real.

Follow each instruction.

1. Nina drew a realistic picture of a tree. Name three or four details that made it realistic.

 ____

 ____

2. A realistic painting is different from a painting that is not realistic. Write the main difference.

 ____

 ____

3. Look at the pictures. Circle the one that is realistic.

4. Write a sentence about something you might draw. Use the word *realistic*.

 ____

 ____

Name ______________________

Compare Words

pottery—Containers made by hand from clay.

sculpture—Works of art made from clay, wood, stone, or metal.

Write *pottery* or *sculpture* on each blank.

1. A stone statue is a ______________. A clay bowl is ______________.

2. An artist carves wood to make a ______________. An artist spins a wheel to shape clay for ______________.

3. Glue toothpicks together to make a ______________ like a tower. Paint a coating on the clay bowl to make ______________ that shines like glass.

4. This vase holds flowers. The vase was made from clay that was shaped and baked. It is a kind of ______________. This ______________ was also made from baked clay. It has the shape of a flower.

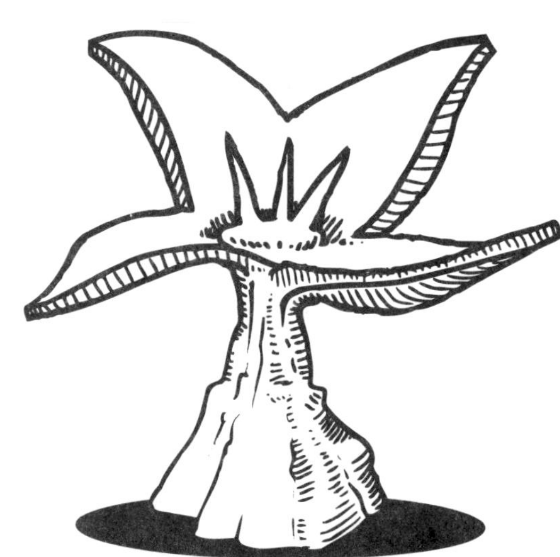

Name ______________________

Make Connections

band—A group that plays music.

compose—To write something, especially music.

instrument—An object used to make music.

musician—A person who plays music.

Complete each sentence with a vocabulary word.

1. A drum is one ______________________.
2. The music teacher will ______________________ a song for us to sing.
3. The ______________________ tapped her feet as she played
4. A piano is a large ______________________.
5. Owen plays the trumpet in the marching ______________________.
6. A ______________________ plays an instrument.

Name ______________________

Make Connections

band	compose	instrument	musician

Read each sentence. Is it correct? Put a ✓ after it. If it is not correct, show how to fix it.

1. A horn and a flute are both bands.

2. The musician blew into the compose.

3. Bands play in musicians.

4. A band is an instrument.

5. A musician could compose a song.

Name ______________________________

Make Connections

Read the paragraph below. Think about the meaning of each **bold** word.

Pedro is learning to play the **guitar**. He started by learning to **pluck** one string at a time. Each string played one **note**. Now, Pedro can play a song. He can **strum** the six strings with one hand and sing a **solo**.

Write the vocabulary word that matches each meaning.

1. ______________________ A sound made by a singer or an instrument.
2. ______________________ A piece of music for one singer or one musician.
3. ______________________ An instrument with strings that are strummed or plucked.
4. ______________________ To play a stringed instrument by passing the fingers over the strings.
5. ______________________ To play a stringed instrument with quick pulls of the strings.

Name ____________________

Make Connections

guitar	note	pluck	solo	strum

Read each sentence. Is it correct? Put a ✓ after it. If it is not correct, show how to fix it.

1. Strum a string with a quick tug.

2. A musician guitars a strum.

3. Every song is made of notes.

4. A guitar has strings to solo and pluck.

5. Three musicians played a solo on guitars.

Name ______________________________

Make Connections

Read the paragraph below. Think about the meaning of each **bold** word.

Look at that **dancer**! Her **costume** has **colorful** ribbons on it. They **twirl** around her as she spins. The dancer can **balance** on one foot. She can **stretch** her other foot high into the air. Would you like to dance like her?

Write the vocabulary word that matches each meaning.

1. ______________________ To turn around very fast.
2. ______________________ A person who dances.
3. ______________________ Clothes worn by an actor or a dancer.
4. ______________________ To hold the body in place without falling.
5. ______________________ Having bright colors
6. ______________________ To push out an arm, leg, or other body part as far as it can go.

Name ______________________

Make Connections

balance	colorful	costume	dancer	stretch	twirl

Read each sentence. Is it correct? Put a ✓ after it. If it is not correct, show how to fix it.

1. Hold your arms by your sides to stretch them.

2. Stand very still to twirl on one foot.

3. A costume is something to eat.

4. When you balance, you fall down.

5. A black costume is colorful.

6. Dancers twirl and leap to music.

Name ______________________

Make Connections

actor—A person who has a part in a play or movie.

cast—All the actors in a play or movie.

director—A person in charge of the actors and action in a play or movie.

rehearse—To practice a play before putting it on for an audience.

scenery—The painted background on a stage.

stage—The raised area where actors put on a play.

Write a vocabulary word on each blank to complete the paragraphs.

Mr. Grayson has planned every scene of the play. He is the (1.) ______________________. Mr. Grayson has helped each (2.) ______________________ to speak with feeling. He has shown the actors how to move across the (3.) ______________________. There are five actors in the (4.) ______________________. They have practiced their parts for weeks. Painters and builders have put together the (5.) ______________________.

The actors put on their costumes. They (6.) ______________________ the play for the last time. Tonight, they will perform for an audience.

Name ______________________

Make Connections

actor	cast	director	rehearse	scenery	stage

Read each sentence. Is it correct? Put a ✓ after it. If it is not correct, show how to fix it.

1. The cast of a play is the scenery.

2. Scenery is at the back of a stage.

3. Actors perform on a stage.

4. Actors rehearse their cast.

5. Actors tell directors how to speak and move.

6. A director helps actors rehearse.

Name ______________________

Play With Words

Code Words

Choose the word that fits in each sentence. Circle its letter.

1. Who ___ that piece of music?
   a composed
   b patterned
   c stretched

2. A hat might be part of a ___.
   r costume
   s scenery
   t pottery

3. A ___ is like a leader.
   s dancer
   t director
   u sculpture

4. Guitars are ___.
   h musicians
   i instruments
   j strums

5. A play has scenery and a ___.
   q band
   r note
   s cast

6. Sing a ___ alone.
   r rehearse
   s balance
   t solo

Write the circled letters in order. You will find a word to complete the sentence.

A painter, a musician, an actor, or a dancer is an ______________________.

Name ______________________

Play With Words

Vocabulary Search

Read each meaning. Which vocabulary word matches that meaning? Write it on the line. Then, find the word in the puzzle. The words go across and down.

1. Repeating shapes and colors ______________
2. To spin ______________
3. Clay vases, jars, and bowls ______________
4. Lifelike ______________
5. To practice before performing ______________
6. To tug on a string ______________

A	H	P	U	M	E	D	G	O	L	B	N
R	E	A	L	I	S	T	I	C	R	E	I
E	M	C	K	F	O	H	A	P	D	W	G
H	S	I	E	L	B	R	N	U	V	C	X
E	Y	Q	O	P	A	T	T	E	R	N	I
A	T	D	W	O	M	J	W	S	Y	T	A
R	O	N	R	T	A	M	I	F	L	N	P
S	U	S	B	T	I	V	R	S	Q	M	H
E	T	G	R	E	E	P	L	T	U	W	R
L	R	A	N	R	T	J	D	E	V	C	A
O	V	I	Z	Y	P	E	W	O	I	S	N
H	A	T	F	L	G	E	P	L	U	C	K

Game Ideas and Suggestions

Use games and activities to help students better hear, see, and remember content-area vocabulary words. The suggestions on these pages can be used with the words in this book and with any other vocabulary words that students are learning.

Charades

Choose about ten vocabulary words. Write the words on slips of paper and display them. Give students time to think about the words before removing the slips. Then, divide the group into two teams. One team member chooses a slip, holds up fingers to indicate the number of syllables, and pantomimes the word. Teammates try to guess the word within a certain time limit.

Word Art

Help students select vocabulary words to depict as art. Encourage them to use letter shapes and arrangements to indicate what the words mean. Prompt students with questions, such as "How might you arrange the letters of the word *sphere*?" "What might happen to the letters in *magnetic*?"

Vocabulary Word-O

Reproduce and distribute the Vocabulary Word-O game card on page 119 to each student. Write 20 vocabulary words on slips of paper, and display the slips. Have each student choose 9 words to write on his or her card. Shuffle the slips, and choose one slip at a time. Instead of reading the word aloud, offer two clues about it. For example, for the word *location*, you might start with the content area. "This is a geography word." Then, use a strong context sentence, with "blank" for the word. "The 'blank' of our school is on Third Street between Maple Avenue and Oak Street.'" Students should check off the word if it is on their grids. The first student to complete three across, down, or diagonally calls out "Word-O" and reads aloud the three words.

Acrostic Poem

Have students write the letters of a vocabulary word in a column. Help them to tell about the word in a poem in which each line begins with a listed letter. Example for *vote*:

Valuable right
Our chance to have a say
Time to choose
Elect the best person.

Card Pairs

Use index cards cut in half to prepare a deck of 52 cards. Write 26 vocabulary words and 26 synonyms or short definitions on the cards. The cards can be used in a variety of games, such as Memory or Concentration. Below is a suggestion to get you started.

- **Go Fish!** for 2 to 5 Players
- Each player is dealt five cards. Remaining cards are placed face down in

a pile.

- The player to the right of the dealer starts by setting aside any pairs. Then, he or she asks the player on the right for a card needed to make a pair. "Do you have *musician*?" Or "Do you have the meaning of *musician*?"
- If the holder has the requested card, he or she hands it over. If the holder does not have it, the player must "go fish" and draw the top card from the pile. If no match can be made, the next player takes a turn.
- The winner is the first player with no cards in hand or the player with the most pairs after all cards have been drawn.

Word Hunt

Emphasize that vocabulary words appear in print and online in a variety of informational resources. As you come across a vocabulary word—in a headline, advertisement, or another resource—save the printed source or make a printout. Challenge students to read the text with you and identify the vocabulary word. Discuss what the word means in the provided context.

Dictionary Guess

Have one student randomly choose a word from the Student Dictionary and read the definition aloud to the group. Partners or small groups then try to write the vocabulary word that matches the definition. Continue until each student has had a chance to choose a word and read its definition aloud. A point is awarded for each correct word.

Racetrack Games

Have students design their own racetrack board games or make one from a template you provide, such as the template on page 120. Here is one way to use the template.

- Select 20 vocabulary words for students to write in the spaces.
- Make a small cardboard spinner by drawing a circle divided into three sections labeled 1, 2, and 3. The "spinner" can be a paper clip attached to a paper fastener.
- Provide small objects for students to use as markers.
- Each player spins, and the highest number goes first.
- A player spins and moves the marker the number of spaces shown. The player must say the word on the space and demonstrate knowledge of it by giving its definition or using it in a good context sentence.
- Players may use a dictionary to check the player's response. A player who is not correct loses a turn.
- The first player to reach the finish line wins.

WORDO!

Finish

Start

______________________'s

Student Dictionary

Important Math Words I Need to Know!

add (ad) *verb* To put two or more numbers together. *Add 3, 5, and 7 to get 15.*

bar graph (bar graf) *noun* A chart that uses bars to stand for amounts.

cent (sent) *noun* One penny, written as 1¢, or $.01.

cube (kyoob) *noun* A shape made of six squares put together. *Put an ice cube in the glass.*

difference (DIF rins) *noun* The answer after subtracting. *Subtract 4 from 10 to get a difference of 6.*

estimate (ES tuh mayt) *verb* To tell about how many. *noun* A good guess about how much or how many.

even number (E vun NUM bur) *noun* A number that can make pairs. The numbers 0, 2, 4, 6, and 8 are even numbers.

dime *noun* A coin worth ten cents, written as 10¢, or $.10.

dollar (DOL lur) *noun* Paper money worth 100 cents, written as $1.00.

measure (MEZH ur) *verb* To find out how long, big, or heavy something is. *Use a ruler to measure length in inches.*

minus (MY nus) *noun* The sign (–) that tells to subtract. *preposition* Less. *Six minus five is one.*

nickel (NIK ul) *noun* A coin worth five cents, written as 5¢ or $.05.

odd number (od NUM bur) *noun* A number that cannot make pairs. The numbers 1, 3, 5, 7, and 9 are odd numbers.

pictograph (PIK tuh graf) *noun* A chart that uses pictures to stand for amounts.

plus *noun* The sign (+) that tells to add. *preposition* Added to. *Six plus five is eleven.*

quarter (KWOR tur) *noun* A coin worth 25 cents, written as 25¢ or $.25.

regroup (ree GROOP) *verb* To show the same number in a different way by trading ones and tens, tens and hundreds, and so on. *One way to regroup 35 is to change 3 tens to 2 tens and 10 ones.*

sphere (sfeer) *noun* The shape of a ball.

subtract (sub TRAKT) *verb* To take away one number from another. *Subtract 20 from 30 to get 10.*

sum *noun* The answer after adding numbers. *The sum of 3, 5, and 7 is 15.*

More Math Words I Need to Know:

Important Science and Health Words I Need to Know!

amphibian (am FIB ee un) *noun* A frog, toad, salamander, or other animal that has smooth skin and lives where it is wet or moist. Amphibians spend the first part of their lives in water. They get air from the water through gills.

attract (uh TRAKT) *verb* To pull things closer. *A magnet attracts iron.*

breathe (breeth) *verb* To take in air and blow it out. *We breathe air into our lungs.*

constellation (kon stuh LAY shun) *noun* A group of stars seen from the Earth. People have always named constellations after animals and other things formed by connecting imaginary lines between the stars.

flower (FLOU ur) *noun* The male and female parts of a plant. The flower makes seeds that grow into new plants.

fruit (froot) *noun* The part of a plant that holds the seeds.

heart (hart) *noun* The organ in the chest with muscles that pump blood throughout the body.

larva (LAR vuh) *noun* The form of an insect just after hatching. A larva usually looks like a worm. The name for more than one larva is *larvae* (LAR vee).

life cycle (life SY kul) *noun* The changes in any living thing from its start to its adult form. Fish, birds, and many other animals lay eggs. An egg is the first stage of the animal's life cycle.

lung *noun* One of a pair of organs in the chest that help the body take in oxygen and get rid of carbon dioxide.

magnetic (mag NET ik) *adjective* **1.** Able to stick to a magnet. **2.** Having the quality of a magnet.

magnify (MAG nih fy) *verb* To make something seem larger. *A telescope and binoculars are tools that magnify objects.*

mammal (MAM ul) *noun* An animal with hair on its skin. A mother mammal feeds her young with milk from her body.

moon *noun* A natural object in space that travels around a planet. *The Earth has only one moon, but other planets have many moons.*

muscle (MUS ul) *noun* A tissue in the body that can squeeze and relax again and again. *The bones move because they are pulled by muscles.*

offspring *noun* The young of animals. *The offspring of birds depend on their parents for food.*

oxygen (OK sih jin) *noun* A gas in

the air. *People need oxygen to live.*

planet (PLAN it) *noun* An object in space that travels around a star. Earth and Jupiter are two of the planets that travel around the Sun.

pole *noun* The north or south end of a magnet.

pump *verb* To force a gas or a liquid to move. *The heart pumps blood.* *noun* Something that pumps. *The heart is a pump.*

pupa (PYOO puh) *noun* The stage in an insect's life when it is inside a cocoon or other case. *A pupa appears to be at rest and does not eat.*

repel (rih PEL) *verb* To push things away. *Like poles of a magnet repel each other.*

reptile (REP tile) *noun* A snake, alligator, turtle, or other animal with an outer covering of scales or plates. Some reptiles live in water, but all breathe air.

root *noun* The part of a plant that is underground. Roots collect water from the soil and bring it to the plant.

seedling *noun* A plant that has begun to grow from a seed. *A seedling poked up from the ground.*

soil *noun* The tiny pieces of rock, rotting material, and living things that make up the top layer of the Earth.

solar system (SOH lur SIS tim) *noun* The Sun and all the bodies that travel around it. Planets and their moons are some of the bodies in our solar system.

sprout *verb* To start to grow from a seed or to start to grow buds.

stem *noun* The long main part of a plant. Buds grow from the stem.

trait (trayt) *noun* A body feature or behavior. *Two traits of that dog are long fur and a friendly manner.*

More Science and Health Words I Need to Know:

____

____

____

____

____

____

Important Technology Words I Need to Know!

communication (kuh MYOON ih kay shun) *noun* Sending and receiving messages. *The phone and the radio are two machines used for communication.*

construction (kun STRUK shun) *noun* Building something. *Stone, steel, and wood are some materials used in construction.*

cursor (KUR sur) *noun* The blinking bar on the computer screen that marks the place to type.

delete (dih LEET) *verb* To get rid of text or pictures in a computer file.

desktop *noun* The display on the computer screen of a background and small pictures of programs and files.

file *noun* Information that is stored under a single name. *Computer files are inside folders.*

hardware *noun* The parts of a computer system. *The monitor, keyboard, and printer are hardware.*

insert (in SURT) *verb* To add text or pictures at a particular point on a page displayed on the computer screen.

manufacture (man yuh FAK chur) *verb* To make things in a factory.

monitor (MON ih tur) *noun* The part of the computer that has the screen.

problem (PROB lum) *noun* Something that needs to be solved.

scroll (skrohl) *verb* To make text and pictures move up, down, left, or right on a computer screen.

software *noun* The programs that run on a computer.

solution (suh LOO shun) *noun* A way to solve a problem. *Machines make work easier and are solutions to many problems.*

transportation (trans por TAY shun) *noun* Moving people and things from one place to another. *Ships are used for water transportation.*

More Technology Words I Need to Know:

Important Language Arts Words I Need to Know!

alphabetical order (al fuh BET ik ul OR dur) *noun* ABC order. Words or names in alphabetical order are listed by their first letters.

author (AW thur) *noun* Someone who writes a story, an article, or a book.

capitalize (KAP it uh lize) *verb* To begin a word with an uppercase, or capital, letter. *Capitalize the first word in a sentence.*

cause-effect (KAWZ uh FEKT) *noun* The connection between an event and the reason for it. The effect is what happens, and the cause is why it happens.

chapter (CHAP tur) *noun* A section of a book. The chapters in a book are numbered.

character (KAH rik tur) *noun* A person or an animal in a story.

compound word (KOM pound wurd) *noun* A word made of two smaller words. The words *baseball*, *sidewalk*, and *everyone* are compound words.

consonant (KON suh nint) *noun* A letter or a sound that is not a vowel. The consonant letters are *b*, *c*, *d*, *f*, *g*, *h*, *j*, *k*, *l*, *m*, *n*, *p*, *q*, *r*, *s*, *t*, *v*, *w*, and *y* as in *yellow*.

contraction (kun TRAK shun) *noun* A word made by shortening two words. An apostrophe ' stands for one or more missing letters. *In the contraction don't, the apostrophe stands for the missing letter* o *in* do not.

description (dih SKRIP shun) *noun* Words that tell about what something is like. Descriptions help readers picture something, hear it, touch it, taste it, and smell it.

detail (dih TAYL) *noun* A piece of information. *Add details to make your description clear and interesting.*

exclamation point (eks kluh MAY shun point) *noun* The mark at the end of a sentence that shows strong feeling. This sentence ends with an exclamation point!

heading (HED ing) *noun* A title for a section of information. *This chapter on snakes has several headings, including "How Snakes Shed Their Skin."*

illustrator (IL uh stray tur) *noun* Someone who draws pictures for a story, an article, or a book.

main idea (mayn ie DEE uh) *noun* The most important idea about the topic of a paragraph or a section.

paragraph (PAR uh graf) *noun* A group of sentences about one main idea. A paragraph begins on a new line. The first word of a paragraph is indented—it begins with blank space.

period (PEER ee ud) *noun* The dot that marks the end of a sentence. This sentence ends with a period.

phonics (FON iks) *noun* The connections between letters and their sounds.

play *noun* A story for actors.

poem (POH im) *noun* A piece of writing set out in lines. A poem is meant to be read aloud. The lines have a beat, and words may rhyme.

prediction (prih DIK shun) *noun* A good guess about what will happen next in a story or what a book will be about.

question mark (KWES chun mark) *verb* The mark at the end of a sentence that asks a question. Does this sentence end with a question mark?

rhyme (rime) *verb* To have the same ending sounds. *The words* blue, too, *and* shoe *rhyme. noun* The same ending sounds.

sentence (SEN tins) *noun* A group of words that shows a complete thought. A sentence begins with a capital letter and ends with a period or other end mark.

setting (SET ing) *noun* Where and when a story takes place.

strategy (STRAT uh jee) *noun* Steps to take to read with understanding. *If you come to a word you don't know, one strategy is read the sentence again and look for clues to word meaning.*

summary (SUM uh ree) *noun* A shortened form of a story or an article. A summary gives only the most important ideas and information.

syllable (SIL uh bul) *noun* A word or part of a word with only one vowel sound. *The word* ham *has one syllable,* hammer *has two syllables, and* hammering *has three.*

table of contents (TAY bul uv KON tents) *noun* A list of the chapters in a book.

vowel (VOU ul) *noun* The letters *a*, *e*, *i*, *o*, *u* and their sounds. The letter *y* is a vowel in words such as *silly*, *gym*, and *cry*.

More Language Arts Words I Need to Know:

____

____

Important History Words I Need to Know!

celebration (sel uh BRAY shun) *noun* A kind of party held to remember a special and happy event. *The Fourth of July is a celebration with picnics and fireworks.*

colony (KOL uh nee) *noun* A group of people from one land who live and work together in a new land.

community (kuh MYOO nih tee) *noun* A group of people who live in the same area.

event (ih VENT) *noun* Something that happens. *The storm was a terrible event for the city.*

future (FYOO chur) *noun* Times that have not happened yet.

heroism (HEHR oh iz um) *noun* The actions of a hero, or brave person.

legend (LEJ und) *noun* A story first told long ago. A legend is usually based on real people, events, or places, but most of the details are made up.

liberty (LIB ur tee) *noun* Freedom.

modern (MOD urn) *adjective* Of the present time. *Computers are modern machines.*

nation (NAY shun) *noun* A country. *The United States is a nation made of fifty states.*

past *noun* Times that have gone by.

present (PREZ int) *noun* Times we are living in. The present is the time after the past and before the future.

symbol (SIM bul) *noun* A picture or thing that stands for an idea. *A dove is a symbol of peace.*

Thanksgiving (thangks GIV ing) *noun* The holiday of Thanksgiving Day, held in the United States on the fourth Thursday in November. The holiday recalls a historic event at Plymouth, Massachusetts, in the fall of 1621. The Pilgrims who had survived a terrible winter feasted with Native Americans and gave thanks for their blessings.

timeline *noun* A line that shows events in order of time.

More History Words I Need to Know:

Important Geography Words I Need to Know!

bay *noun* A part of the sea that reaches a wide curve of shore.

coast (kohst) *noun* Land that meets the sea.

direction (dih REK shun) *noun* The way in which something moves or points.

east (eest) *noun, adjective, adverb* Toward the right side of a world map.

globe (glohb) *noun* The Earth shown on a ball.

grid *noun* Lines that cross a map to help readers find a location. *Our house is at C–5 on the grid of our town map.*

island (IE lind) *noun* Land surrounded by water.

legend (LEJ und) *noun* The key to the symbols on a map.

location (loh KAY shun) *noun* Where on the Earth a place is found. *This map shows the location of Lake Boone.*

north *noun, adjective, adverb* Toward the top of a world map.

northeast (north EEST) *noun, adjective, adverb* A direction halfway between north and east.

northwest (north WEST) *noun, adjective, adverb* A direction halfway between north and west.

ocean (OH shun) *noun* Any of the largest bodies of salt water on the Earth.

route (root) or (rout) *noun* The path from one location to another. *The route from home to school goes by the playground.*

rural (RUR ul) *adjective* Having to do with country life. *This rural area has many farms.*

south *noun, adjective, adverb* Toward the bottom of a world map.

southeast (south EEST) *noun, adjective, adverb* A direction halfway between south and east.

southwest (south WEST) *noun, adjective, adverb* A direction halfway between south and west.

urban (UR bun) *adjective* Having to do with city life. *This urban area has crowded streets.*

west *noun, adjective, adverb* Toward the left side of a world map.

More Geography Words I Need to Know:

Important Civics and Economics Words I Need to Know!

buyer (BY ur) *noun* Someone who buys something with money.

citizen (SIT ih zin) *noun* A person born in a country or who becomes a member of that country.

elect (ih LEKT) *verb* To pick someone by voting. *We elected Gabe our class president.*

election (ih LEK shun) *noun* The event at which people vote for someone. *The United States holds an election for president every four years.*

goods *plural noun* Things for sale.

govern (GUV urn) *verb* To lead a city, state, or country.

government (GUV urn mint) *noun* A group that makes laws and sees that they are obeyed.

governor (GUV ur nur) *noun* The leader of a state's government.

honesty (ON uh stee) *noun* Telling the truth and acting in a sincere way.

justice (JUS tis) *noun* Fair treatment according to laws or ideas of fairness.

law *noun* A rule that everyone must follow.

mayor (MAY ur) *noun* The leader of a city's government.

needs *plural noun* Things that people must have to live. *Food, clothing, and a home are basic needs.*

president (PREZ ih dent) *noun* The leader of a country's government.

price (prise) *noun* How much money is paid for something.

purchase (PUR chis) *verb* To buy something.

product (PROD ukt) *noun* Something that is made or grown for sale.

responsibility (rih SPON suh bil uh tee) *noun* An action that someone must take. *Everyone has the responsibility to obey laws.*

rights (rites) *plural noun* Basic freedoms. *We have the right to speak freely.*

seller (SEL ur) *noun* Someone who sells a product or a service.

service (SUR vis) *noun* Work that a person does for someone. *A bus driver provides a service.*

state (stayt) *noun* An area that makes up part of a country and has its own government. *Alaska and Texas are the two biggest states in the United States.*

tax (taks) *noun* Money paid to the government.

vote *verb* To make a choice to decide who will win an election or to decide on an action.

wants (wonts) *plural noun* Things that people would like to have. *After we have paid for our needs,* *we might have money left over to pay for our wants.*

More Civics and Economics Words I Need to Know:

Important Art Words I Need to Know!

actor (AK tur) *noun* A person who has a part in a play or movie.

balance (BAL uns) *verb* To hold the body in place without falling. *Hold your arms out to help you balance on one foot.*

band *noun* A group that plays music. *Some bands play rock music.*

cast (kast) *noun* All the actors in a play or movie.

colorful (KUL ur ful) *adjective* Having bright colors. *The clown has colorful clothes.*

compose (kum POHZ) *verb* To write something, especially music.

costume (KOS tyoom) *noun* Clothes worn by an actor or a dancer. *The children dressed in animal costumes for the play.*

dancer (DAN sur) *noun* A person who dances.

director (dih REK tur) *noun* A person who directs, or takes charge of, the actors and action in a play or movie.

guitar (gih TAR) *noun* A musical instrument with strings and a long neck. It is played by strumming and plucking.

instrument (IN struh mint) *noun* An object used to make music. Guitars, drums, and flutes are instruments.

musician (myoo ZISH un) *noun* Someone who plays or composes music.

note (noht) *noun* A sound made by a singer or an instrument.

pattern (PAT urn) *noun* Lines, colors, or shapes that repeat to make a design. *Stripes, polka dots, and checks are a few patterns in cloth.*

pluck (pluk) *verb* To play a stringed instrument with quick pulls of the strings. *The musician plucked one string of the violin.*

pottery (POT uh ree) *noun* Containers made by hand from clay.

realistic (ree uh LIS tik) *adjective* In a way that seems real. *The artist painted a realistic scene of woods.*

rehearse (rih HURS) *verb* To practice a play or music before performing for an audience.

scenery (SEE nuh ree) *noun* The painted background on a stage. The scenery in a play shows the audience where the action is taking place.

sculpture (SKULP chur) *noun* A work of art made from clay, wood, stone, or metal. *The stone sculpture shows the head of a woman.*

solo (SOH loh) *noun* A piece of music for one singer or one musician.

stage (stayj) *noun* The raised area where actors put on a play. *The curtains opened to show the stage.*

stretch (strech) *verb* To push out an arm, leg, or other body part as far as it can go. *You can stretch your body by reaching for the sky.*

strum *verb* To play a stringed instrument by passing the fingers over the strings. *The musician strummed his banjo and sang.*

twirl (twurl) *verb* To turn around very fast. *The dancer's skirt spread out as she twirled.*

More Art Words I Need to Know:

Notes

Answer Key

Math

Page 6

1. Ruben's estimate is better. There are about 20 second graders in a class, not 100.
2. $6.00
3. about 4 glasses left
4. Sentences will vary.

Page 7

1. odd number; even number
2. even number; odd number
3. even number; odd number

Page 8

1. s; **2.** cross out; **3.** c; **4.** s; **5.** c; **6.** cross out; **7.** cross out; **8.** s; **9.** c; **10.** cross out

Page 9

1. plus; **2.** add; **3.** sum; **4.** add; **5.** sum; **6.** plus

Page 10

Students' corrections will vary.
1. The plus sign looks like a cross.
2. Add numbers to find the sum.
3. Checkmark
4. Six cookies plus four cookies makes ten cookies.
5. Adding makes a number bigger.

Page 11

1. minus; **2.** subtract; **3.** regroup; **4.** minus; **5.** subtract; **6.** difference

Page 12

Students' corrections will vary.
1. Regroup 1 ten and 9 ones as 19 ones.
2. Checkmark
3. Subtract numbers to find the difference.
4. Checkmark
5. Checkmark

Page 13

1. Nine children chose sliding. The pictograph shows 3 pictures for Slide, and each one stands for 3 children.
2. Dillon kicked the farthest. The bar graph shows that the bar for Dillon is the highest—35 feet.
3. Sample response: Maybe someone marked the spot where the ball landed. Then, someone used a yardstick to measure the distance from the starting point.

Page 14

Students' corrections will vary.
1. Checkmark
2. You can measure your height with a tape measure.
3. The longest bar in a bar graph shows the biggest amount.
4. A pictograph might have one picture standing for five people.
5. Use feet or meters to measure the length of a room.

Page 15

1. cent; **2.** dime; **3.** nickel; **4.** dollar; **5.** quarter; **6.** nickel; **7.** dime; **8.** quarter; **9.** cent

Page 16

Students' corrections will vary.
1. Two nickels and a dime make $.20.
2. Checkmark
3. Seventy-five dollars is written $75.00.
4. A dime is worth more than a nickel.
5. Two quarters are the same as five dimes.

Page 17

1. $.15 + $.20 = $.35
2. Bar for Meg should reach 6; bar for Jaden should reach 9; bar for Rico should reach 7.
3. Sample response: 54 = 50 + 4 = 40 + 14
4. Sample response: 10 (even) – 1 = 9 (odd)
5. Sample response: I estimate that my desk is about 20 inches wide. I could use a ruler to measure its exact width.

Page 18

Answers spell *number*.

Science and Health

Page 20

Sample responses:
1. Baby mammals are born alive, and baby birds hatch from eggs.
2. Mammals have hair, and fish have scales.
3. elephant, mouse
4. Sentences will vary.

Page 21

1. feather, ant, grain of sand
2. Sample response: Use binoculars or a camera with a zoom lens.
3. Sample response: The lines in the leaf are magnified.
4. Sample response: I would like to magnify a strand of hair to see what it looks like up close.

Page 22

1. flower; **2.** fruit; **3.** fruit; **4.** flower; **5.** flower; **6.** fruit

Page 23

1. reptile; **2.** amphibian; **3.** amphibian; **4.** reptile; **5.** reptile; **6.** reptile

Answer Key

Page 24
1. attract; **2.** magnetic; **3.** pole; **4.** repel;
5. magnetic; **6.** attract

Page 25
Students' corrections will vary.
1. Checkmark
2. A magnet will attract something that is magnetic.
3. Pennies are made of metal, but they are not magnetic.
4. Checkmark
5. A magnet shaped like a horseshoe has one south pole and one north pole.

Page 26
1. planet; **2.** moon; **3.** constellation; **4.** solar system

Page 27
Students' corrections will vary.
1. Jupiter is a planet, and it has moons.
2. Checkmark
3. A moon travels around its planet.
4. Stars form a constellation.
5. A constellation is a group of stars.

Page 28
1. seedling; **2.** stem; **3.** root; **4.** root; **5.** sprout;
6. soil

Page 29
Students' corrections will vary.
1. A plant's roots are below the stem.
2. Water travels from the roots up the stem.
3. A seedling sprouts from soil.
4. Checkmark
5. Checkmark

Page 30
1. larva; **2.** offspring; **3.** life cycle; **4.** pupa;
5. traits

Page 31
1. pupa; **2.** larva; **3.** life cycle; **4.** offspring;
5. larva; **6.** traits

Page 32
1. oxygen; **2.** breathe; **3.** pumps; **4.** muscles;
5. heart; **6.** lungs

Page 33
1. muscles; **2.** lungs; **3.** oxygen; **4.** breathe;
5. heart; **6.** pump

Page 34
Answers spell *nature*.

Technology

Page 36
Sample responses:
1. ball, cap
2. wood, metal
3. flowerpot (manufactured), plant (not manufactured)
4. Sentences will vary.

Page 37
1. problem, solution; **2.** solution, problem;
3. problem, solution

Page 38
1. communication; **2.** transportation;
3. communication; **4.** construction;
5. construction; **6.** transportation (or construction)

Page 39
Students' corrections will vary.
1. Checkmark
2. Workers have different jobs in the construction of a building.
3. Checkmark
4. One form of communication is television.
5. Freight trains are important in the transportation of food.

Page 40
1. file; **2.** software; **3.** hardware; **4.** software;
5. file; **6.** monitor

Page 41
Students' corrections will vary.
1. Checkmark
2. A computer mouse is hardware.
3. Click on a file to open it.
4. Checkmark
5. A computer file is software.

Page 42
1. desktop; **2.** cursor; **3.** delete; **4.** scroll; **5.** insert

Page 43
1. desktop; **2.** delete; **3.** cursor; **4.** insert; **5.** scroll;
6. cursor

Page 44
Sample responses:
1. telephone, radio
2. to find things on the Web
3. a wagon you pull yourself
4. Bridge builders use strong materials like steel.
5. Sample response: If you have a problem, try to think of a solution.
6. Captioned drawings will vary.

Answer Key

Page 45
Answers spell *laptop*.

Page 46
1. manufacture; **2.** hardware; **3.** software;
4. solution; **5.** delete; **6.** desktop

Language Arts

Page 48
Sample responses:
1. orange, pink, huge, tiny, round
2. loud, clanging sound; prickly, tingling touch; spicy, peppery taste; fresh, sweet smell
3. Captioned drawings will vary.
4. Sentences will vary.

Page 49
1. Sample responses: Lightning strikes a tree; The tree burns to the ground.
2. Allies's belly hurts (effect); She ate too much ice cream (cause)
3. Sample response: The car's flat tire was caused by a nail in the street.
4. Sample response: The snow melted (effect) because the sun came out (cause).

Page 50
1. illustrator **2.** illustrator; **3.** author; **4.** author;
5. illustrator; **6.** author

Page 51
Compound Words: can not, some where, your self, fire wood, thunder storm
Contractions: do not, we are, you are, would not, they have

Page 52
1. table of contents; **2.** rhyme; **3.** play; **4.** poem;
5. play; **6.** chapter

Page 53
Students' corrections will vary.
1. We wore masks to perform our play.
2. The words *fast* and *past* rhyme.
3. A book has chapters.
4. A table of contents lists the poems in a book.
5. Checkmark

Page 54
1. keep; **2.** Elly, Fred, Rob; **3.** time; **4.** screamed;
5. The word *cup* begins with a *c* that sounds like *k*;
6. fat

Page 55
Students' corrections will vary.
1. Use alphabetical order to put the name *James* before the name *Pam*.
2. The word *hop* has one syllable.
3. There is one vowel in the word *bump*.
4. Checkmark
5. Put your lips together and hum to make the consonant sound *mmmm*.

Page 56
1. sentence; **2.** exclamation point; **3.** period;
4. capitalize; **5.** question mark; **6.** capitalize

Page 57
1. add exclamation point
2. capitalize *Eddie*
3. Sample response: We all should play outside. sentence
4. add question mark
5. add period

Page 58
1. setting; **2.** predictions; **3.** strategy; **4.** character

Page 59
1. setting; **2.** character; **3.** strategy; **4.** prediction;
5. character; **6.** strategy

Page 60
1. paragraph; **2.** main idea; **3.** heading; **4.** details;
5. summary

Page 61
1. main idea; **2.** summary; **3.** heading; **4.** paragraph; **5.** detail; **6.** paragraph

Page 62
Answers spell *needle*.

History

Page 64
Sample responses:
1. The flag has red and white stripes. In one corner is a blue box with 50 white stars in it. The stars stand for the 50 states. The flag stands for the United States.
2. A symbol of an eagle is on the back of a one-dollar bill. The eagle is the national bird of the United States.
3. Captioned drawings will vary.
4. Sentences will vary.

Answer Key

Page 65
Sample responses:
1. A legend about George Washington is a made-up story about him. A book of information gives facts about his life.
2. In a fairy-tale, magical things happen. A legend could be based on something that really happened.
3. *The Legend of Johnny Appleseed*; the book tells about a man who planted apple trees for Americans traveling west to build new homes.
4. Sentences will vary.

Page 66
1. past; **2.** past; **3.** present; **4.** present; **5.** past; **6.** present

Page 67
1. future; **2.** timeline; **3.** modern; **4.** future; **5.** event; **6.** timeline

Page 68
Students' corrections will vary.
1. A modern house looks new.
2. Important events will happen in the future.
3. Checkmark
4. Checkmark
5. A timeline shows past events.

Page 69
1. nation; **2.** liberty; **3.** heroism; **4.** heroism; **5.** nation; **6.** liberty

Page 70
Students' corrections will vary.
1. An act of heroism is an unusual event.
2. Ghana is a nation in Africa.
3. Checkmark
4. Checkmark
5. The Statue of Liberty welcomes people to the United States.

Page 71
1. Thanksgiving; **2.** colony; **3.** community; **4.** celebration

Page 72
Students' corrections will vary.
1. The best-known Thanksgiving food is turkey.
2. A celebration is a happy event.
3. A big city has many communities.
4. Before the United States became a nation, it was made of thirteen colonies.
5. Checkmark

Page 73
Sample responses:
1. Pilgrim hats
2. a parade with floats
3. the United States, Canada, Mexico
4. The people who lived in the United States wanted their own nation, not ruled by Britain.
5. The legend of Pocahontas tells how she showed heroism by saving John Smith's life.
6. Captioned drawings will vary.

Page 74
Answers spell *museum*.

Geography

Page 76
Sample responses:
1. It is shaped like a ball. It shows the land and water as they are on the Earth.
2. to find out where different countries are; to plan a trip around the world
3. Responses will vary, but students should recognize the United States.
4. The travelers visited cities in many countries of the world.

Page 77
Sample responses:
1. Look at a map. Ask for directions.
2. Responses will vary but, students should note the street.
3. Star at intersection of Fifth Street and Montrose Avenue
4. Sentences will vary.

Page 78
1. rural; **2.** rural; **3.** urban; **4.** urban; **5.** rural; **6.** urban

Page 79
1. route; **2.** legend; **3.** grid; **4.** route; **5.** legend; **6.** grid

Page 80
Students' corrections will vary.
1. A map legend is a key to symbols.
2. A route could be curved, crooked, or straight.
3. Checkmark
4. Look at the legend to understand the symbols on a map.
5. What is your route from home to school?

Page 81
1. west; **2.** north; **3.** direction; **4.** south; **5.** east; **6.** east

Answer Key

Page 82
Students' corrections will vary.
1. Checkmark
2. Run your finger down a map of the world to go south.
3. If you are facing east, the direction west is behind you.
4. Canada is north of the United States.
5. ...That direction is east.

Page 83
1. southeast; **2.** northeast; **3.** southwest; **4.** northwest

Page 84
Students' corrections will vary.
1. The direction northeast is halfway between north and east.
2. Checkmark
3. The state of Florida is in the southeast of the United States.
4. The direction southwest is toward the left and bottom of a world map.
5. ...That direction is southeast.

Page 85
1. ocean; **2.** island; **3.** ocean; **4.** bay; **5.** coast; **6.** island

Page 86
Students' corrections will vary.
1. An island is surrounded by water.
2. Islands are found in all bodies of water.
3. Checkmark
4. Checkmark
5. A bay lies along a coast.

Page 87
1. Sample response: A map is flat, and a globe is round.
2. north, northeast, east, southeast, south, southwest, west, northwest
3. Captioned drawings will vary.
4. cross out legend; it is only on a map, not on the Earth
5. Sentences will vary.

Page 88
Answers spell *global*.

Civics and Economics

Page 90
Sample responses:
1. The person tells the truth, so you can believe what you're told.
2. I'm so sorry I lost your doll. I left it outside, and now it's gone. I'll save my money to buy you another one.
3. left picture might be labeled *dishonesty* or *lying*; right picture should be labeled *honesty*.
4. Sometimes you might want to lie so that you won't be punished for doing something wrong, but telling the truth is the right thing to do.

Page 91
Sample responses:
1. A teacher should show justice and treat everyone the same.
2. A person who has been treated unfairly wants justice.
3. Justice means giving each side equal weight and treating both sides fairly.
4. just (fair); justice (fairness)

Page 92
1. need; **2.** want; **3.** need; **4.** want; **5.** need; **6.** need

Page 93
1. service; **2.** goods; **3.** service; **4.** goods; **5.** goods; **6.** service

Page 94
1. right, responsibility; **2.** right, responsibility; **3.** responsibility, right

Page 95
1. citizen; **2.** election; **3.** law; **4.** vote; **5.** elect; **6.** vote

Page 96
Students' corrections will vary.
1. Checkmark
2. All American citizens have the right to vote.
3. Checkmark
4. We counted the votes to see who won the election.
5. People voted in the last election.

Page 97
1. govern; **2.** government; **3.** governor; **4.** mayor; **5.** president; **6.** state

Page 98
Students' corrections will vary.
1. The leader of a city is a mayor.
2. The leader of a state is a governor.
3. Checkmark
4. There are fifty states in the United States.
5. The government of the United States is based in Washington, D.C.
6. Checkmark

Answer Key

Page 99
1. price; **2.** tax; **3.** seller; **4.** purchase; **5.** buyer; **6.** product

Page 100
Students' corrections will vary.
1. Workers pay a tax to the government.
2. The price of this carton of juice is $2.50.
3. Checkmark
4. If you purchase a product, you are a buyer.
5. Most buyers like lower prices.
6. Checkmark

Page 101
Answers spell *nation*.

Page 102
1. mayor; **2.** justice; **3.** president; **4.** government; **5.** election; **6.** goods

The Arts

Page 104
1. Sample response: a plaid pattern
2. wallpaper, snowflakes, a rug
3. Captioned drawings will vary.
4. Sample response: ...the repeating designs are interesting.

Page 105
1. Sample response: It had a brown trunk, many branches, green leaves, and seemed as big as a real tree.
2. Sample response: A realistic painting looks like a real person, place, or thing. A painting that is not realistic does not look like real life.
3. The third picture is circled.
4. Sentences will vary.

Page 106
1. sculpture, pottery; **2.** sculpture, pottery; **3.** sculpture, pottery; **4.** pottery, sculpture

Page 107
1. instrument; **2.** compose; **3.** musician; **4.** instrument; **5.** band; **6.** musician

Page 108
Students' corrections will vary.
1. A horn and a flute are both instruments.
2. The musician blew into the instrument.
3. Musicians play in bands.
4. A band is a group of musicians.
5. Checkmark

Page 109
1. note; **2.** solo; **3.** guitar; **4.** strum; **5.** pluck

Page 110
Students' corrections will vary.
1. Pluck a string with a quick tug.
2. A musician strums a guitar.
3. Checkmark
4. A guitar has strings to strum and pluck.
5. One musician played a solo on a guitar.

Page 111
1. twirl; **2.** dancer; **3.** costume; **4.** balance; **5.** colorful; **6.** stretch

Page 112
Students' corrections will vary.
1. Hold your arms out from your sides to stretch them.
2. Stand very still to balance on one foot.
3. A costume is something to wear.
4. When you balance, you do not fall down.
5. A red costume is colorful.
6. Checkmark

Page 113
1. director; **2.** actor; **3.** stage; **4.** cast; **5.** scenery; **6.** rehearse

Page 114
Students' corrections will vary.
1. The cast of a play is the actors.
2. Checkmark
3. Checkmark
4. Actors rehearse their parts.
5. Directors tell actors how to speak and move.
6. Checkmark

Page 115
Answers spell *artist*.

Page 116
1. pattern; **2.** twirl; **3.** pottery; **4.** realistic; **5.** rehearse; **6.** pluck

Math **difference**	Math **estimate**	Math **measure**
Math **minus**	Math **plus**	Math **sum**
Science and Health **larva**	Science and Health **life cycle**	Science and Health **lungs**

To find out how long, big, or heavy something is.

To tell about how many.

The answer after subtracting.

The answer after adding numbers.

1. The sign (+) that tells to add. **2.** Added to.

1. The sign (–) that tells to subtract. **2.** Less.

The pair of organs in the chest that help the body take in oxygen and get rid of carbon dioxide.

The changes in any living thing from its start to its adult form.

The form of an insect just after hatching. It usually looks like a worm.

Science and Health **magnetic**	Science and Health **magnify**	Science and Health **mammal**
Science and Health **oxygen**	Science and Health **planet**	Science and Health **solar system**
Technology **communication**	Technology **manufacture**	Technology **software**

An animal with hair on its skin. The mother animal feeds her young with milk from her body.

To make something seem larger.

1. Able to stick to a magnet.
2. Having the quality of a magnet.

The Sun and all the bodies that travel around it.

An object in space that travels around a star.

A gas in the air that people need to live.

The programs that run on a computer.

To make things in a factory.

Sending and receiving messages.

Technology **transportation**	Language Arts **capitalize**	Language Arts **character**
Language Arts **consonant**	Language Arts **contraction**	Language Arts **illustrator**
Language Arts **prediction**	Language Arts **setting**	Language Arts **summary**

A person or an animal in a story.

To begin a word with an uppercase, or capital, letter.

Moving people and things from one place to another.

Someone who draws pictures for a story, an article, or a book.

A word made by shortening two words. An apostrophe (') stands for one or more missing letters.

A letter or a sound that is not a vowel.

A shortened form of a story or an article. It gives only the most important ideas and information.

Where and when a story takes place.

A good guess about what will happen next in a story or what a book will be about.

Language Arts **vowel**	History **celebration**	History **colony**
History **liberty**	History **nation**	History **present**
Geography **coast**	Geography **island**	Geography **location**

A group of people from one land who live and work together in a new land.

A kind of party held to remember a special and happy event.

The letters *a, e, i, o, u* and their sounds, and the letter *y* in words such as *silly, gym,* and *cry*.

Times we are living in. It comes after the past and before the future.

A country.

Freedom.

Where on the Earth a place is found.

Land surrounded by water.

Land that meets the sea.

Geography **route**	Geography **rural**	Geography **urban**
Civics and Economics **citizen**	Civics and Economics **election**	Civics and Economics **govern**
Civics and Economics **justice**	Civics and Economics **mayor**	Civics and Economics **president**

Having to do with city life.

Having to do with country life.

The path from one location to another.

To lead a city, state, or country.

The event at which people vote for someone.

A person born in a country or who becomes a member of that country.

The leader of a country's government.

The leader of a city's government.

Fair treatment according to laws or ideas of fairness.

Civics and Economics **product**	Civics and Economics **responsibility**	Civics and Economics **rights**
The Arts **costume**	The Arts **instrument**	The Arts **musician**
The Arts **pattern**	The Arts **rehearse**	The Arts **sculpture**

Basic freedoms.

An action that someone must take.

Something that is made or grown for sale.

Someone who plays or composes music.

An object used to make music, such as a guitar, a drum, or a flute.

Clothes worn by an actor or a dancer.

A work of art made from clay, wood, stone, or metal.

To practice a play or music before performing for an audience.

Lines, colors, or shapes that repeat to make a design.